January 2012

More Praise for Kouzes and Posner's *Credibility*

"If you have been searching for the one book this year that will help you become a more effective leader, you have found it. Kouzes and Posner have done it again: gone straight to the heart of the matter. Developing and sustaining credibility is the core task of effective leaders in today's organizations, and this revised edition of *Credibility* provides fresh insight, practical wisdom, and relevant examples for managers everywhere on how to become such a leader. Like your own leadership GPS, *Credibility* provides the essential roadmap for managers everywhere on how to establish, enhance, and maintain the trust and followership of your constituents."

—Michael Burchell, corporate vice president, Great Place to Work® Institute; coauthor, *The Great Workplace: How to Build It, How to Keep It, and Why It Matters*

"We are living in a time of extraordinary challenges—economic, political, environmental, and even familial. But we'll never resolve these looming challenges if we can't trust our leaders. We don't know of a better book than this one for those leaders who really want to gain and hold the credibility to lead people forward."

—Jennifer Granholm, former Governor of the State of Michigan, and Dan Mulhern, Haas School of Business, University of California, Berkeley

"In *Credibility*, Jim Kouzes and Barry Posner have done something unique and important. They have uncovered the very essence of why we follow some leaders enthusiastically and yet reject others of apparently equal or even greater ability. But this is just the beginning. Through worldwide research, they have answered the critically important question of whether the same characteristics, among different cultures, are equally important for leading. You cannot read this book and apply its lessons without acquiring a much deeper understanding and greater capacity to lead. I highly recommend it."

—William A. Cohen, PhD, Major General, USAFR, Retired; author, *Drucker on Leadership and Heroic Leadership*

Credibility

Credibility

How Leaders *Gain* and *Lose* It

WHY PEOPLE DEMAND IT

JAMES M. KOUZES

BARRY Z. POSNER

JOSSEY-BASS
A Wiley Imprint
www.josseybass.com

Published by Jossey-Bass
A Wiley Imprint
989 Market Street, San Francisco, CA 94103-1741—www.josseybass.com

Jossey-Bass books and products are available through most bookstores. To contact Jossey-Bass directly call our Customer Care Department within the U.S. at 800-956-7739, outside the U.S. at 317-572-3986, or fax 317-572-4002.

Jossey-Bass also publishes its books in a variety of electronic formats. Some content that appears in print may not be available in electronic books.

Library of Congress Cataloging-in-Publication Data
Kouzes, James M., 1945-
  Credibility : how leaders gain and lose it, why people demand it / James M. Kouzes,
Barry Z. Posner. – 2nd ed.
      p. cm.
  Includes bibliographical references and index.
    ISBN 978-0-470-65171-1 (hardback), 978-1-118-09837-0 (ebk),
978-1-118-09838-7 (ebk), 978-1-118-09839-4 (ebk)
1. Leadership. 2. Executive ability. 3. Interpersonal relations.   I. Posner, Barry Z.
II. Title.
  HD57.7.K678 2011
  658.4'092–dc22

                                                                    2011011132

Printed in the United States of America

HB Printing   10 9 8 7 6 5 4 3 2 1

We're pleased to dedicate this volume to some exceptionally credible colleagues—Warren Bennis, Ken Blanchard, Irwin Federman, John Gardner, Frances Hesselbein, and Warren Schmidt. In working with them over the years we've benefited greatly from their wise counsel and keen insights, and it is with deep gratitude that we recognize them publicly.

CONTENTS

On Credibility
and the Restoration
of Trust and Confidence

Credibility is the foundation of leadership. This is the inescapable conclusion we have come to after more than thirty years of research into the dynamics of the relationship between leaders and constituents. People have to believe in their leaders before they will willingly follow them. That's why we first wrote *Credibility: How Leaders Gain and Lose It, Why People Demand It* twenty years ago, and it's why we have taken the time to thoroughly update and revise it.

Credibility is about how leaders earn the trust and confidence of their constituents. It's about what people demand of their leaders as a prerequisite to willingly contributing their hearts and minds to a common cause, and it's about the actions leaders must take in order to intensify their constituents' commitment.

Timing is everything. When the first edition of *Credibility* was published in 1993 we noted that nearly half of America's workforce was cynical. Worldwide, 60 percent or more of workers believed that their management wasn't honest with them, more than half had lost confidence in the abilities of their top management, and overall confidence in major business was at a historic low of only 26 percent.[1] We wanted to remind leaders how important it was to attend to the fundamentals. We thought they should take the importance of earning and sustaining credibility more seriously. We wanted to offer a useful framework and practical suggestions on what leaders could do to increase the trust and confidence others had in them. We hoped we could play some small part in restoring people's faith in their leaders.

For several years, it seemed that leaders were listening. Things got better—perhaps because leaders took notice, or perhaps because things couldn't get much worse. The public's mood changed. The decade of the nineties and the turn of the century saw increases in trust, confidence, and credibility among leaders of major institutions. But these shifts turned out to be short-lived.

In 2010, during a cab ride to the airport in Flint, Michigan, we were chatting with the driver, a laid-off automotive worker. He was telling us that he once had a great job on the assembly line at a nearby General Motors plant, but that now he and his buddies were convinced that they wouldn't find another manufacturing job. He told us how he was worried that they'd never be able to return to the lifestyle they once enjoyed. Then he said, "How can it be that GM lost $38 billion in 2007 and then in the first quarter of 2010 they made $1 billion in profits? They must have been hiding the money!"

We could hear the anger and cynicism in his voice. He was clearly suspicious of the company, and it was evident that he spoke for more than himself. He was expressing something, he said, that his friends, family, and former coworkers had discussed quite often. While his numbers may not be entirely accurate, his mood was unmistakable.

After rising for a decade, in the early 2000s confidence in institutions and leaders began to slide, and by 2007 trust (the key ingredient of credibility) took a nosedive. Whatever gains had been achieved had been lost.[2] Organized religion, Wall Street, Congress, business executives, the presidency, public schools, newspapers, banks, insurance companies, car salespeople, HMOs, and more have taken hits. No single incident accounts for the whole decline, but many point to Enron as the beginning of the fall. WorldCom, Tyco, Fannie Mae, other corporate accounting scandals, and illegal trading in mutual funds confirmed the suspicions of many about corporate greed, with folks like Bernard Madoff and Calisto Tanzi of Italy's Parmalat only reinforcing these fears. Sex scandals surfaced in churches, as well as in the halls of Congress and statehouses. A housing and mortgage crisis in the United States, with a corresponding collapse in the financial markets, set in motion a prolonged economic recession that had the potential for bankrupting countries around the globe. Millions lost their jobs; millions lost the roof over their heads; millions watched helplessly as the value of their retirement savings dwindled or disappeared. Adding to the anger of ordinary people was the fact that once-powerful organizations were given government bailouts while at the same time paying massive bonuses to their top executives. To exacerbate the misery, in recent years environmental disasters have ruined communities and cost jobs in already fragile economic regions. And to top it all off, the politicians on the campaign trail proclaimed in their political ads that their opponents were liars, instead of offering solutions that might help. The net result was that public trust in all politicians declined.

It's no shock, then, that institutional trust, confidence, and credibility once again all hit new lows. And along with it interpersonal trust has also declined, even more than trust in institutions.[3] People are growing more reluctant to believe in their coworkers and their neighbors, especially in highly diverse organizations and communities where people are unfamiliar with the norms and expectations of their colleagues.

Many wonder if there are any leaders left who have the strength of character to sustain their trust. Substantial numbers of people believe that leaders lack the capability to guide business and governmental institutions to greatness in this intensely turbulent and competitive global marketplace. There is the gnawing sense in many corridors that leaders are not competent to handle the tough challenges; that they are not telling the truth; and that they are motivated more by greed and self-interest than by concerns for the customer, the employees, or the country.

Admittedly, opinions about the people who occupy leadership positions tend to rise and fall with current events.[4] When times are good, people exhibit more confidence in their leaders, and when times are bad they exhibit less. The more severe the events and the more compressed the time frame, the more cynical people are likely to become. It is natural to expect, then, in a prolonged recession—with attendant layoffs and shrinking family incomes—that the credibility of business, labor, and government leaders would decline. A natural suspicion of power, a host of unrealistically positive expectations, and the confluence of events setting off the worldwide economic crisis beginning in late 2007 can explain a great deal about why leaders have lost credibility. Bad timing can often ruin credibility as much as bad actions.

But dismissing credibility problems as simply a function of the times permits leaders to escape responsibility for their own actions. The entire economic system is based on trust. It's not based on a particular investment model, price-earnings ratio, income statement, or balance sheet. It's not based on any of these rational concepts. It's based on whether people *believe* in the numbers and in the people who are supplying them. If people don't trust those who handle their money, their livelihoods, and their lives, they'll just refuse to participate. Leaders must accept that it is their responsibility to take the first step in earning back what has been lost and then further steps to sustain it.

So what can leaders do now to restore trust and confidence? What positive actions can leaders take to strengthen credibility over time? What can you do? What can anyone do? These are the questions we answer in this book.

Our Research into Credibility

Much has been written about what leaders do to get extraordinary things done, but little has been written about leadership from the constituent's point of view. There are a few books and articles about being a good follower, but we have not been satisfied with the perspective they present. These turbulent times require energized *constituents* who enthusiastically participate in the process and take up the call for more leadership at all levels. So we thought it was essential to look into the specific behaviors constituents need from a leader if they are to become fully engaged in and committed to a leader's call to action.

Credibility is the result of an intensive, ongoing investigation. In writing this book, we have relied upon our own surveys, which over the years have been administered to well over 100,000 people from around the world. The data reported in *Credibility* is from our continuing study, and, as we note later, the results have not varied since we began our research in the early 1980s.

In addition, we have accumulated more than double the number of written case studies since the first edition of this book, and they now total well over a thousand. Along with our students, we have also conducted hundreds of in-depth interviews with individuals "admired as leaders" in order to deepen our understanding of and gather personal stories about the key actions and behaviors of credible leaders.

From the surveys, we identified the qualities people *most* looked for in those individuals they would be *willing* to follow; from the case studies and interviews we identified specific actions that give leaders credibility. Focus groups and subject-matter experts helped us define and refine the most significant behaviors. Further survey research projects, both within and across organizations, enabled us to validate the importance of these leadership actions and to determine empirically that credibility makes a difference in work attitudes and performance.[5]

Who Should Read This Book?

With *Credibility* we continue our commitment to assist people in all parts of the globe, at all levels, and in all types of organizations—public, private, educational, religious, voluntary, governmental, military, and not-for-profit settings—in furthering their abilities to lead others to get extraordinary things done. Therefore, in the course of writing this book we collected data from aspiring and experienced organizational managers (from all functions and sectors), as well as community leaders, volunteer leaders, religious leaders, political leaders, labor leaders, and student leaders. After more than thirty years of research, we are more convinced than ever that leadership is everyone's business. Consequently, we believe *Credibility* will be of interest to anyone—whether at work, at home, or in social and volunteer activities—who wishes to step forward and guide people to places they have never been before, to new personal, organizational, and social futures.

As a result of reading this book, you will learn

- The qualities that constituents look for and admire in leaders, the people whose direction they would willingly follow
- The foundation of leadership and of all working relationships
- The principles and disciplines that strengthen leadership credibility
- Actions you can take immediately to apply the practices to your own leadership initiatives
- The struggles leaders face in living up to their constituents' expectations

In short, you will learn how credibility is the foundation of leadership and, in fact, of all relationships that work. And you will also learn that credibility is measured not by you but by those you lead.

What's New and What's Not

This second edition of *Credibility* is a completely revised and slimmed-down version of the original. In addition to the worthy goal of saving the planet some paper, we trimmed the length for several reasons. First, we sharpened the focus on our central theme: how leaders earn and sustain credibility. In the first edition, we took detours into issues of service quality, for example, which, while important, weren't directly on message. Second, technology now allows us to move some of what we had written to the cloud. You will find material on our research, for example, at www.leadershipchallenge.com/go/credibility. Third, we developed an entirely new companion volume to accompany this book. *Strengthening Credibility: A Leader's Workbook* provides many developmental and application exercises for building and sustaining credibility.

This new edition of *Credibility* has a longer and broader reach than the earlier book. Our research is global, and the cases in this edition reflect that. From Asia and Australia to Europe, the Middle East, and North and South America, we show how people around the world affirm that credibility is the foundation of leadership.

All the cases in this book have been updated, and 90 percent of them are new to this volume. They are fresh illustrations of the changing nature of the context in which people now work. Part of that new context is a more open organizational environment—due in part to the globalization of the economy, the increased use of social media, and the rise of a whole new generation of younger leaders. This edition reflects this changing landscape.

What's not new is our intense interest in how values clarification and culture creation are at the top of a leader's agenda. Some of our earliest research clearly showed that commitment, satisfaction, productivity, and other positive outcomes were significantly higher when people shared the values of their organizations. This finding is reaffirmed in our most current studies.[6]

As our research evolved we discovered that unless *personal* values were clear it really didn't matter how clear the organization's values were. People don't get more committed to a company or to a cause because the organization nails its credo to the door. They get more committed because it matters to them.

During the past three decades, we've continued to ask another fundamental question, "What do you look for and admire in a leader, someone whose direction you would *willingly* follow?" You might expect we'd get a different set of responses over this period of time. After all, people keep telling us that the world is radically different today from what it was in the eighties.

But we haven't heard a different answer. No matter whom we've asked and no matter where we've asked it, *credibility* is still *the foundation of leadership*. In fact, given what the world has been going through these past few years, this lesson is even more relevant today.

Overview of the Contents

In Chapter One, "Leadership Is a Relationship," we present our view that leadership is a relationship between those who aspire to lead and those who choose to follow. We also describe the results of our long-term research projects to identify the qualities people most look for and admire in their leaders, and we explain how the data clearly indicate that credibility is the foundation of leadership.

In Chapter Two, "Credibility Makes a Difference," we discuss the positive influence credible leaders have on people and organizations and the negative impact that low-credibility leaders have on morale and performance. Through anecdotes and examples from the leaders and constituents in our studies, we bring the research findings to life. Then we introduce the idea that earning and sustaining credibility requires six disciplines, which we explain in the next six chapters.

In Chapter Three, "Discover Your Self," we talk about how the credibility journey begins with the process of self-discovery—with an inner exploration of credos, competence, confidence, and character. Credos are your guides, competence provides the skills to enact your credos, and self-confidence gives you the will to behave in a way that is consistent with your beliefs. The sum of it all is character.

In Chapter Four, "Appreciate Constituents," we show that leaders are seen as trustworthy when they have their constituents' best interests at heart. To strengthen credibility, leaders explore others' aims and aspirations. Credible leaders learn to listen and to listen well. They appreciate the hopes and dreams of their diverse constituencies.

In Chapter Five, "Affirm Shared Values," we discuss why it is so important for credible leaders to integrate diverse viewpoints into unifying themes. We present our findings that shared values make a significant difference in the health of individuals, organizations, and communities. We talk about how leaders can find common ground, build community, and resolve conflicts on the basis of principles, not position.

In Chapter Six, "Develop Capacity," we observe that people cannot act on the values they espouse unless they have the knowledge, skills, and resources to do so. Credible organizational leaders continuously develop the capacity of their organizations to put values into practice.

They educate, offer choices, inform, foster self-confidence, and create a climate for lifelong learning. In short, they liberate the leader in everyone.

Constituents do not serve leaders; leaders serve constituents. Both serve a common purpose. In Chapter Seven, "Serve a Purpose," we examine ways that credible leaders demonstrate their personal commitment to the shared values and visions of the organization. They stay in touch with constituents, are the first to accept responsibility, spend time on the important values, teach others, and hold themselves accountable.

In Chapter Eight, "Sustain Hope," we examine how credible leaders attract constituents by lifting people's spirits and restoring belief in the future. They sustain hope by taking charge and demonstrating the courage of their convictions, by arousing positive thoughts and images, and by seeking and giving support. Credible leaders keep hope alive—which is a critical task since, in the end, only people with hope achieve greatness.

In Chapter Nine, "The Struggle to Be Human," we discuss the tensions leaders grapple with as they try to respond to constituents while remaining true to their own beliefs. We also identify some excesses of leadership and of expectation and offer antidotes for dealing with these tensions. Building and strengthening credibility is an ongoing struggle, and we remind you in this final chapter and in the brief Epilogue following that the life you live is the legacy you leave behind.

You Make a Difference

Leadership matters. And it matters even more in uncertain times than it does in stable times. Organizations and communities certainly have their share of turbulence right now. You can expect many more massive and wrenching changes in the years to come. Adversity and hardships test leaders, and they test followers, too. These times call for bold actions and risky moves, often without predictable outcomes. You will have to ask your constituents to change, to transform, to do things differently. And the only thing they will have is your word that this is the right thing to do.

Success in initiating or responding to change is inextricably linked to the credibility of those leading the efforts. Constituents will commit to the extent that they believe in those guiding the change. It is wise, therefore, for leaders to begin every significant change with a "credit check." It's not just "Do my constituents believe that the new system will improve our performance?" Or even "Do they believe that this risky policy is for the greater good?" It's also "Do they believe in me and my ability to lead this effort?"

But you can't do it alone. Neither can your organization, your community, or your country. Everyone—leaders and constituents alike—shares responsibility for getting extraordinary things done. You need every constituent's energetic involvement as much as constituents need your courage of conviction. You need to make leadership everyone's business, not just your business.

We all contribute to the renewal of mutual trust and understanding. By making leadership about *us* and not about *them*, we all take responsibility for doing what we say we will do. And, in the end, everyone becomes more credible.

James M. Kouzes
Barry Z. Posner
May 2011

CHAPTER ONE

Leadership Is a Relationship

"Although it was probably subconscious, I did not readily admit to my friends where I worked," Beth Bremner told us. "I just used to say, 'A big bank.'" The reason, she said, "predominantly had to do with the fact that I did not believe that our leaders were acting with the integrity and honesty that I hold so dear to my heart. I did not feel management set the kind of example that I wanted to abide by."

Beth, South African by birth, was educated in the U.K. She holds an MBA from the Hong Kong University of Science and Technology and has worked throughout Europe, the Middle East, and Asia.[1] But Beth's sentiment is one that we hear time and time again all over the globe. Beth wants what the vast majority of people want from their leaders and their organizations:

> I want to work for a company where I believe in the message being passed down from my top management team. I want to feel as though I am part of the team and that I have the same beliefs as the company does. I have learned that one needs to love what one does and believe that one is doing a good job for a great company. My best performance will never be ensured by feeling like a cog in the wheel of a company for a salary. I want to work

1

in a company where I can share the direction and vision of
my leaders. I have learned that most individuals are driven by the
same thing as I . . . the possibilities that surround us and being
excited about the future and what it holds.

Beth is right. The same things drive most people. They are energized
by values and visions that give their lives meaning and purpose. They
want to be surrounded by something that uplifts and excites them. And
it is also clear that the thousands of professionals like Beth have certain
expectations of their leaders. They won't commit themselves to work
harder and more effectively for just anyone.

Leadership may once have been conferred by rank and privilege. It
may once have been something that was characterized by a command-
and-control, top-down, do-as-I-say style. But no more. Those days are
long gone. Today, leadership is only an aspiration. It is something you
have to earn every day, because on a daily basis, people choose whether
or not they're going to follow you. It's something you keep striving to
achieve and never assume you've fully attained.

The old organizational hierarchy just can't generate the kind of
commitment that's required in our global society. This isn't a call
for open elections inside organizations. But managers should not kid
themselves. People do vote—with their energy, with their dedication,
with their loyalty, with their talent, with their actions. Don't you put
forth higher-quality effort when you believe that the people leading you
are there to serve your needs and not just their own interests?

Leadership is a relationship between those who aspire to lead and
those who choose to follow. Any discussion of leadership must attend to
the dynamics of this relationship. Strategies, tactics, skills, and practices
are hollow and fruitless unless the fundamental human aspirations that
connect leaders and their constituents are understood and appreciated.

So, what do constituents expect from leaders? What do leaders expect from constituents? What purpose do leaders serve? Why do people believe in some leaders but not in others? Why do some people choose to follow one leader while others reject that leader? What actions sustain the relationship? What actions destroy it? What is the state of the current relationship between leaders and constituents? These are the questions that intrigued us and that drove the research behind this book. We wanted to understand more deeply what formed the foundation of a constructive and positive relationship between constituents and their leaders, and what leaders needed to do to build and sustain that kind of relationship. Organizations and communities cannot be renewed and revitalized, nor can towering institutions even be dreamed about, until these and related questions are answered.

Consider what the late John Gardner—former cabinet secretary, founder of Common Cause, adviser to six U.S. presidents, and respected author and scholar—had to say about all this:

> A loyal constituency is won when the people, consciously or unconsciously, judge the leader to be capable of solving their problems and meeting their needs, when the leader is seen as symbolizing their norms, and when their image of the leader (whether or not it corresponds to reality) is congruent with their inner environment of myth and legend.[2]

From his decades of experience in working with some of the most powerful people in the world, John learned that people willingly follow the direction of someone who is attuned to their aims and aspirations, worries and fears, ideals and images. He also found that ultimately the constituents are the arbiters of the quality of leadership they receive. In the end, leaders don't decide who leads. Followers do.

Loyalty is not something a boss (or anyone for that matter) can demand or even command. It is something the people—the constituency—choose to grant to a leader who has earned it. The people's choice is based not upon authority but upon the degree to which the leader lives up to the expectations constituents hold.

Leadership is something one experiences in an interaction with another human being. That experience varies from leader to leader, from constituent to constituent, and from day to day. No two leaders are exactly alike, no two constituent groups are exactly alike, and no two days in the life of leaders and constituents are exactly alike. And even in this digital age, when face-to-face contact seems to be diminishing—and this change is the source of many of the leadership problems being experienced these days—it is the interaction between leaders and constituents that turns opportunities into successes.

The key to unlocking greater leadership potential can be found when you seek to understand the desires and expectations of your constituents and when you act on them in ways that correspond to their image of what an exemplary leader is and does.

The Characteristics of Admired Leaders

We began our investigation into what people expected from their leaders more than three decades ago, in a study sponsored by the American Management Association. We asked the open-ended question, "What values (personal traits or characteristics) do you look for in your superiors?"[3] (As you can see, we were stuck in the old hierarchical metaphors back then.)

More than 1,500 managers nationwide provided 225 values, characteristics, and traits that they believed to be crucial in the people leading them. A panel of researchers and managers subsequently analyzed the

225 factors and reduced them to 15 categories. Of those, the most frequent categories, in order of mention, were

1. *Integrity* (is truthful, is trustworthy, has character, has convictions)
2. *Competence* (is capable, is productive, is efficient)
3. *Leadership* (is inspiring, is decisive, provides direction)

A follow-up study involving more than 800 senior public sector administrators replicated these findings.[4]

In subsequent studies, we broadened the categories, elaborated on the earlier findings, and improved the research methodology. We eventually produced a twenty-item survey checklist, which became part of the research protocol for this book. Over the years, more than 75,000 people around the globe have completed the "Characteristics of Admired Leaders" checklist. People select from the twenty characteristics (or qualities) listed after this paragraph the seven that they most "look for and admire in a leader, someone whose direction you would *willingly* follow." Pause for a moment and make a mental note of the seven that would be on your own list.

Characteristics of Admired Leaders

- Ambitious (aspiring, hardworking, striving)
- Broad-minded (open-minded, flexible, receptive, tolerant)
- Caring (appreciative, compassionate, concerned, loving, nurturing)
- Competent (capable, proficient, effective, gets the job done, professional)
- Cooperative (collaborative, team player, responsive)
- Courageous (bold, daring, gutsy)
- Dependable (reliable, conscientious, responsible)
- Determined (dedicated, resolute, persistent, purposeful)
- Fair-minded (just, unprejudiced, objective, forgiving, willing to pardon others)

- Forward-looking (visionary, foresighted, concerned about the future, sense of direction)
- Honest (truthful, has integrity, trustworthy, has character)
- Imaginative (creative, innovative, curious)
- Independent (self-reliant, self-sufficient, self-confident)
- Inspiring (uplifting, enthusiastic, energetic, humorous, cheerful, positive about the future)
- Intelligent (bright, smart, thoughtful, intellectual, reflective, logical)
- Loyal (faithful, dutiful, unswerving in allegiance, devoted)
- Mature (experienced, wise, has depth)
- Self-Controlled (restrained, self-disciplined)
- Straightforward (direct, candid, forthright)
- Supportive (helpful, offers assistance, comforting)

Our research also includes more than 1,000 written case studies of "My Most Admired Leader," in which people responded to questions about leaders with whom they had personal experience and for whom they had great admiration and respect. From these case studies we collected specific examples of actions of respected leaders, information on the affective nature of admired leader–constituent relationships, and profiles on the types of projects or programs involved. This information came from sources in North and South America, Europe, Asia, and Australia. Focus groups further enabled us to determine the behaviors of admired leaders. Finally, a series of empirical studies provided further insights into the leadership actions that specifically influence people's assessments of credibility.[5]

Additionally, in-depth interviews with more than 150 managers revealed the qualities they looked for and admired in their leaders and why. These richly detailed, colorful anecdotes and specific examples brought the survey data to life. From all of this data we developed a framework for describing the actions that admired leaders take to build a special kind of leader-constituent relationship, one that not only leaves a lifelong impression but builds community and makes a significant performance difference.

The results of our studies over the last three decades have been strikingly consistent. They have remained consistent not only over time but also around the world and across categories of age, gender, ethnicity, functional discipline, organizational level, and the like. People are remarkably clear about the qualities leaders must demonstrate if they want others to voluntarily enlist in a common cause and to freely commit to action.

What are these crucial attributes? According to our empirical data, the majority of people look for and admire leaders who are honest, forward-looking, inspiring, and competent. Take a moment to examine the data from these surveys. The results from the most current sample are displayed in the left-hand column of Table 1.1. Also shown are the accumulated results from two prior reports in 2002 and 1987.

As you can see, these four characteristics—honest, forward-looking, inspiring, and competent—rank well above the rest. And this is true not just today but has been over several decades as well. The same is true around the globe, as Table 1.2 shows. While the exact rank order (first through fourth) might vary from country to country, these same four qualities remain at the top of the list of what people everywhere want from their leaders.

Honest

In virtually every survey, honesty is selected more often than any other leadership characteristic. No matter where the studies have been conducted—regardless of country, geographical region, or type of organization—the most important leadership attribute since we began our research in 1980 has always been honesty.

7

TABLE 1.1 Characteristics of Admired Leaders (Percentage of People Selecting Characteristic Over the Years)

Characteristic	2010	2002	1987
Honest	85	88	83
Forward-looking	70	71	62
Inspiring	69	65	58
Competent	64	66	67
Intelligent	42	47	43
Broad-minded	40	40	37
Dependable	37	33	32
Supportive	36	35	32
Fair-minded	35	42	40
Straightforward	31	34	34
Determined	28	23	20
Cooperative	26	28	25
Ambitious	26	17	21
Courageous	21	20	27
Caring	20	20	26
Imaginative	18	23	34
Loyal	18	14	11
Mature	16	21	23
Self-Controlled	11	8	13
Independent	6	6	10

Honesty is absolutely essential to leadership. If people are going to follow someone willingly, whether into battle or into the boardroom, they first want to assure themselves that the person is worthy of their trust. They want to know that the would-be leader is truthful, ethical, and principled. This is exactly the point that Ken Chang, branch manager for Schenker China-BAX Global, made about his general manager: "Whether it is good news or bad news, we'll get it. He keeps us posted on what we are doing and the progress we are making." And

TABLE 1.2 Characteristics of Admired Leaders Around the World (Rank Order by Country)

Country	Honest	Forward-Looking	Inspiring	Competent
United States	1	2	3	4
Australia	1	2	3	4
Brazil	1	2	4	3
Canada	1	2	3	4
China	3	2	1	4
Japan	1[t]	1[t]	4	3
Korea	1[t]	1[t]	4	3
Malaysia	1	2	4	3
Mexico	1	2	3	4
Philippines	1	3	2	4
Scandinavia	3	2	1	4
Singapore	4	2[t]	1	2[t]
South America	1	2	4	3
Turkey	3	1	2	4
United Arab Emirates	1	2	3	4

t indicates a tie in the rank order.

the payoff, as Ken pointed out, is that "when the leader is honest with his followers then we will be honest in return. This helps to form an honest atmosphere in the organization."

The benefits of honesty cannot be overstated. Employees must know they can trust their leader—as they can only do when someone is honest with them. As Anand Reddy, project manager at Intel, explained: "A failure of honesty poisons the team, damages the trust between people, and breaks down team cohesion. Besides, nobody wants to follow a leader who is not honest." For Ian Foo, working as a consultant with Accenture in Australia, the importance of honesty and trust was demonstrated in the way his most admired leader kept his word: "Being honest means that if you make promises to people

9

you never break them. You are only as good as your word: If you cannot deliver, do not offer your word." Honesty earns the respect of others and fosters their confidence that leaders can be trusted to follow through on their commitments.

Forward-Looking

Vani Bhargava, manager of financial accounting and analysis at YouWeb Incubator, learned about the importance of being forward-looking from her most admired leader, who told her that it is "critical to have a vision about how things could be and to be clear enough about it that others will be able to see it themselves." Gloria Leung told us that because her most admired leader at Hang Seng Bank (Hong Kong) is forward-looking, "this provides us the capacity to walk a path towards the future with great confidence, and fosters shared values because we all know where we are heading." "Where people fail as leaders," explained Alex Popovic, director of strategic sales accounts at National Semiconductor, is where they are "myopic in their approach and are unable to communicate the long-term future of the group." "You can't be buried in the details," said Marie Ross, senior manager of EMC's customer reference program. "You have to be looking at the bigger picture." Leaders are expected to have a sense of direction and a concern for the future of the organization. Leaders must know where they are going. They must have a destination in mind when asking others to join them on a journey into the unknown.

It isn't all that surprising that being forward-looking would be so important for senior executives. But the data also indicate that it is very important for frontline supervisors and middle managers as well. If leaders are to be admired and respected, they must have the ability to see across the horizon of time and imagine what might be. People are unwilling to follow those who are directionless. Leaders can be unquestionably

10

honest, but if they don't know where they are going, no one is likely to go any further ahead with them than they themselves can see.

Constituents ask that a leader have a well-defined orientation toward the future. They want to know what the organization will look like, feel like, and be like when it arrives at its goal in six months or six years. They want to have it described to them in rich detail so that they will know when they have arrived and so that they can select the proper route for getting there.

Inspiring

People admire and respect leaders who are dynamic, uplifting, enthusiastic, positive, and optimistic. Claudio Lucero, who led the first South American team's climb to the top of the world's highest mountain, explained: "Dreaming about something is not enough; you have to be able to share that dream and get others to work with you to achieve it." Leaders can't just have dreams of the future; they must be able to communicate those dreams in ways that encourage people to sign on for the duration and to work hard for the goal. In this way they are expected to be inspiring.[6]

Ziya Boyacigiller, serial entrepreneur in the United States and Turkey, testified to the importance of being inspiring. He spoke about the need to "get others to believe so strongly in the vision that they are transformed into followers who are not afraid to fail." The enthusiasm of leaders is contagious and gets everyone to feel that they can make the impossible possible.

Competent

If people are to enlist in another's cause, they must see that individual as capable and effective. Emily Li, APAC finance director at Mindspeed Technologies, described her most admired leader at Efinity in these terms: "He knows what he's doing—he sets goals that are realistic and knows the steps necessary to achieve them—and that creates confidence and motivation in his followers." And, she pointed out, "he knows about how to build upon the expertise of others." The universal expectation is that the leader will be able to get things done for the organizational unit. In this sense, having a winning track record is the surest way to be considered competent.

The type of competence that constituents look for does vary somewhat with the leader's role. For example, leaders who hold officer positions are expected to demonstrate abilities in strategic planning and policymaking. If a new technology challenges the organization, a person more knowledgeable about that technology may be perceived to be a more appropriate leader. A leader on the line or at the point of customer interaction will typically have to be more technically competent than someone removed from day-to-day contact. Yet it is not necessary that the leader have the same level of technical competence as constituents. Much more significant, explained Victor Wang, marketing technical services manager for the Swedish steel company ASSAB Tooling in Dongguan, China, "is that the leader takes the time to learn the business, to know the current operation and everyone in the company, before making changes and decisions."

Expertise in leadership skills per se is another dimension of competence. The abilities to model, inspire, challenge, enable, and encourage—the practices identified over the years in our study of leadership bests and published in our book *The Leadership Challenge*—must be demonstrated if leaders are to be seen as capable.[7]

Consistency Over Time

Honest. Forward-looking. Inspiring. Competent. These four prerequisites to leadership have stood the test of time and geography, even though there have been modest changes in emphasis. For example, in the years since we first collected this data, both *forward-looking* and *inspiring* have increased in importance. More people want their leaders to provide future direction and show uplifting enthusiasm than when we began our research. These times of transition require leaders with the vision and the energy to sustain hope.

Competent remains one of the four most admired characteristics, but it has slightly less importance now than in the past. Some people may be looking more for vision and direction, for inspiration and excitement, than for a track record of getting things done. This shift causes some pause, however, given the increasing complexity of organizations and their environments. It is doubtful that any leader could navigate the white water of today's organization without clear competence, but relative to the original study some people have elected to trade competence for another quality. For instance, *intelligent, broad-minded, supportive*, and *dependable* receive more votes now than ten and twenty years ago.

The quite modest changes in the most-admired rankings underscore the remarkable consistency of people's expectations of leaders over a wide variety of personal, organizational, and cultural dimensions. Nineteen of the twenty leader characteristics have not changed by more than a few percentage points (plus and minus) since the first data was collected in the early 1980s.[8]

Global Leadership and Local Variations

Context matters, and the external environment may influence what people look for and admire in a leader at any given moment or in any specific organization or location. Not that any shifting winds will push people away from seeking leaders who are at their core honest, forward-looking, inspiring, and competent. Over time and across organizations, these four qualities remain the prerequisites to developing yourself as an all-around leader. Yet to be a leader, you must also learn to adapt to and shape your local surroundings. Expectations can vary from organization to organization, function to function, group to group, level to level.

For example, in one particular organization we surveyed, *supportive* was selected as a most admired characteristic by significantly more people (56 percent) than in any other group studied. In this organization, being understanding and helpful was considered dramatically more important by all—whether exempt (salaried) or non-exempt (hourly), male or female, young or old—than in other companies. To be successful in that place, you would have to develop the skills to be supportive along with the skills to demonstrate the other four attributes. In another organization, *courageous* was selected significantly more often than the international norm.

As you might imagine, the differences between the supportive and the courageous organization were palpable. The organizations were as different as night and day, even though each was among the best in its own industry. In academic institutions the percentage of people selecting *intelligent* has been above the norm, while in health care organizations the preference has been *caring*. Among college students *broad-minded* has been more important, and with senior citizens *mature* was selected more often than the norm. But these "local" choices do not take away the majority of votes within each sample population that still go to honest, forward-looking, inspiring, and competent.

People may also see the world a bit differently based on their roles and positions. Managers consistently look for a leader who is *forward-looking*; often fewer than 50 percent of non-managers do. Indeed, the weight given to *forward-looking* goes up in direct proportion to the age and years of work experience of respondents. When it comes to *supportive*, more than 60 percent of exempt employees look for it, while fewer than 40 percent of senior managers do. Professionals in the human resources function are more likely to value supportiveness than are professionals in other disciplines. More women than men tend to value supportive leaders. People in sales tend to value *inspiring* more than those in accounting. Health care professionals place a higher premium on *caring* in their leaders than do those from the manufacturing or engineering sectors. Ethnic minorities often look for more *broad-minded* leaders than do people from the majority ethnic group. Understanding these local differences is important.

If you are likely to rove about as a leader in your career, serving one constituent group today and another tomorrow, it is critical to keep a local perspective without losing or compromising your global understanding. Much as specific attributes may vary from country to country, organization to organization, and function to function, some things remain constant and universal. Honest, forward-looking, inspiring, and competent are those constants. They need to be part of your transportable leadership repertoire. Leaders are expected to carry at least these four qualities with them wherever they go.

Taken singularly, the characteristics of *honest, forward-looking, inspiring*, and *competent* provide a consistently useful guide for leadership selection, action, and development. Taken together, they communicate a more powerful message, one that offers a deeper understanding about the fundamentals of leadership.

Credibility Is the Foundation of Leadership

The characteristics of trustworthiness, expertise, and dynamism compose what communications researchers refer to as "source credibility."[9] In assessing the believability of sources of information—whether the president of the organization, the president of the country, a salesperson, a TV newscaster, or a product spokesperson—those who rate highly on these three characteristics are considered to be credible, believable sources of information.

These three dimensions of source credibility are strikingly similar to three of the most frequently selected qualities in the "Characteristics of Admired Leaders" checklist: *honest, competent*, and *inspiring*. The three factors that explain why a person is a believable source of information—trustworthiness, expertise, and dynamism—are synonyms for three of the top four qualities people look for in a leader they would willingly follow. For trustworthiness, you can say *honest*. For expertise, you can say *competent*. For dynamism, you can say *inspiring*. In other words, what we found quite unexpectedly in our initial research, and what has been reaffirmed since, is that above all else, people want leaders who are *credible*.

People everywhere want to believe in their leaders. They want to have faith and confidence in them as people. People want to believe that their leaders' words can be trusted, that they have the knowledge and skill necessary to lead, and that they are personally excited and enthusiastic about the direction in which they are headed. *Credibility is the foundation of leadership.* As General David Petraeus, commander of the International Security Assistance Force and of U.S. Forces Afghanistan, and tenth commander of the U.S. Central Command, noted,

> There was a point in time when somebody came to me—at the real height of the violence, the most difficult period . . . and candidly there was not much support in certain quarters at that point in time—and said, "Sir, the only thing we have left is your credibility." I took that pretty seriously.[10]

All leaders must take their credibility seriously. Credibility is the foundation on which leaders and constituents will build grand dreams of the future. Without credibility, dreams will die and relationships will rot.

Just think about it this way. Imagine a time when you might need to borrow some money. Imagine that you are trying to get a mortgage to build the house of your dreams, or to open a new business. You sit down across the desk from the loan officer at your local financial services company. After you've completed all the paperwork, the first thing that the loan officer is likely to do is check your credit.

Credit and credibility share the same root origin, *credo*, meaning "I trust or believe." A loan officer checking your credit is literally checking trust and belief, searching to know whether you can make good on your word. The officer wants to know whether to believe you when you say that you will pay the loan back on time and with interest.

When it comes to leaders, in many respects constituents act like loan officers. When leaders make promises (that is, complete verbal promissory notes) about what they will do to guide the organization on a journey to an uplifting new future, people instinctively do a credit check. They ask themselves, "The last time this person made such a promise, did it get kept?" "Was it the truth, or was it just some campaign pledge to get us to sign on?" "Can I trust this person?"

People also ask, "Do I see enough enthusiasm to keep us excited along the difficult road to the future?" "Can this leader inspire others to make the sacrifices necessary to make it through to the end?" And they wonder, "Does this leader have the competence to get us from where we are now to where we'd like to be?" "Does this leader have a track record of accomplishment that would give us confidence for the current effort?"

If the answers to these essential questions—about being honest, inspiring, and competent—are yes, then people are likely to lend their time, talent, and toil willingly. If the answers are no, then people are not likely to voluntarily sign up. Of course, they may go along because they

17

have to (for example, they need this job), but that hardly means that they will take it upon themselves to do more than they must (surely something quite less than their best). When leaders ask others to follow their new strategic directions, their visions of exciting possibilities of a better tomorrow, people first decide whether those leaders can be believed.

Of all the attributes of credibility, however, one is unquestionably of greatest importance. The dimension of honesty accounts for more of the variance in believability than all other factors combined. Being seen as someone who can be trusted, who has high integrity, and who is honest and truthful is essential to being believed. You may know someone who is clearly competent, dynamic, and inspirational, but if you have a sense that that person is not being honest, you will not accept what that person is telling you, and you will not willingly follow. So the credibility check can reliably be simplified to just one question: "Is this person worthy of my trust?"

If your answer is yes, then follow. Even if your endeavor is unsuccessful, you will still respect yourself. If your answer is "I don't know," get more information, and get it fast. But if your answer is no, find another job or find another leader. Even if you are successful, you will not respect yourself. Every time you follow someone you do not trust, you erode your self-esteem: you are diminished in your own and in others' eyes. Your worth depreciates, and you become less valuable to yourself and to others.

Earning Credibility

"You cannot follow someone who isn't credible, who doesn't truly believe in what they're doing—and how they're doing it," said Gayle Hamilton, chief of staff for the senior vice president at Pacific Gas and

Electric. And this viewpoint goes a long way toward explaining why Gayle has always preferred to stay close to those she leads, going back to the decision she made as a division manager to keep her office right next to the train tracks where her crew worked, rather than move to a plusher corporate setting. As she explained: "I don't think people enjoy working for long stretches for someone who won't be part of what's happening."

Leaders like Gayle know that credibility is something that is earned over time. It does not come automatically with the job or the title. It begins early in your life and career, and it is something that you develop day by day, year by year. People tend to initially assume that someone who has risen to a certain status in life, acquired degrees, or achieved significant goals is deserving of their confidence. But complete trust is granted (or not) only after people have had the chance to get to know more about you. The credibility foundation is built brick by brick, stone by stone. And as each new fragment is secured, the support on which you can erect the hopes and dreams of the future is gradually built.

We know that without a firm foundation of personal credibility, leaders can have no hope of enlisting others in a common vision. In this book we concentrate on the solid base on which these visions stand; we do not talk much about the dreams themselves. We focus on the leader's foundation of credibility, because only when it's strong can dreams of the future be supported.

Obviously the loftier and more expansive a leader's dream, the deeper the foundation must be. The less stable the ground underneath, the more solid the foundation must be. Especially in uncertain times, leadership credibility is essential in generating confidence among constituents. Without credibility nothing can be built—at least nothing that can survive the test of time.

19

But does building the foundation warrant the effort? Does credibility really matter? Don't you hear almost daily of business, labor, military, political, and even religious leaders who've become successful, yet who lack credibility? Besides, isn't business about getting results, and if you lack credibility but get good results, then so what? What difference does it make anyway?

It matters a great deal. Despite the evidence that some people can succeed, for a time, in ways that are devious and dishonest, credibility has a significantly positive impact on individual and organizational performance. In the next chapter we examine the difference credibility makes, and what leaders can do to strengthen their credibility.

LEADERSHIP IS A RELATIONSHIP
Key Ideas From Chapter One

- Leadership is a relationship between those who aspire to lead and those who choose to follow.

- People choose to follow a leader not because of a leader's authority but because a leader lives up to the expectations constituents hold.

- The majority of people look for their leaders to be honest, forward-looking, inspiring, and competent.

- Credibility is the foundation of leadership.

- Credibility is earned by daily actions leaders take over time. It does not come automatically with the job or the title.

CHAPTER TWO

Credibility
Makes a Difference

Think about your own personal experiences with individuals you consider to be leaders. These relationships have much to teach you about the difference that people can make in your life—and in the lives of others.[1] Take a moment to think of a time when you willingly followed the direction of someone you admired and respected as a leader. Make some mental or written notes as you answer the following questions:

- What was the situation—the project, program, or activity—in which you were involved with this person? What was the project or activity expected to accomplish?
- What three or four words would you use to describe how you felt when you were involved with this person? How did this leader make you feel about yourself?
- What leadership actions did this person take to get you and others to want to perform at your best? What were the leadership behaviors of this person that you admired?

We've asked these questions of thousands of people. In answering them, Kathy Lacoy, director of operations for a large health care provider, spoke about the time when she was just getting started in her career. Her experience is very representative of what we heard. Her hospital administrator was her most admired leader, someone who continually challenged those around him to expand:

> He always had some kind of new project to work on. He could see what was coming next, something new, something interesting, and something different to do. He taught all the time, all the time. Just in general conversation he was teaching you something, so there was always that opportunity to learn.
>
> He was scrupulously honest so that I had this real trust in him, and I just knew that he would never cause me to be in a situation where I'd sacrifice my ethics or my own personal values or standards....He worked very hard, very long hours....I worked probably the hardest I've worked in my whole life, but I never felt used or abused....He totally trusted me to do my job, wanted to hear feedback, was always available to help problem solve.
>
> And one method of communication—two-way communication—he used was to call floor conferences. These were little meetings...a time for people to be able to ask questions or make suggestions or share their little gripes....He'd take notes while he was doing it, and then get the notes typed up with a response within 24 hours....He was able to take complex issues and synthesize them in terms that people could understand so that everybody shared in the common goal....He set a very high standard.

Kathy said that this leader taught her every day and increased her confidence, often by compliments. One notable way was in introducing her by saying—whether to a visitor or the president of the company—"You're going to have a real treat today. You're going to meet the best damn nurse that ever was." He made it clear that he took a genuine personal interest in Kathy, and in all the employees. And then Kathy related a most dramatic and memorable story of absolute trust:

> I bet nobody ever had a boss that did anything like this. My husband and I had been married for about eight years, had three little kids, and had never had an opportunity to go away for what we call a real vacation. . . . We saved our money—it took a little over six months—and we were going to Acapulco. . . . The day I left, my boss called me into his office and he said, "Now, I don't want to insult you, but I want you to do something. When you go on vacation sometimes, every once in a while, there's something you just really want, but that you know maybe you can't afford, and you feel you shouldn't buy it because you've got three kids that want something else. I'm going to insist that you take with you my American Express card just in case there's anything you really want." Now that's awesome.
>
> People asked me so many times, "How come you have such tremendous loyalty to this company?" It's because of things like that. I mean, I never used that card. . . . He just believed in the inherent self-worth of everyone.

Similar to Kathy's feelings are those of Shankar Ramachandran. He quoted his most admired leader, Steve Dellaporta, as saying, "Honor and respect people, show you care and be genuine, they will do anything for you." And, as Shankar said:

> As his constituent, I can vouch for this when he went above and beyond in helping me with a personal situation. My workplace does not allow people working offsite, and Steve went all the way to the top to get me permission so I could work from India for three months, and spend time with my dad who had just been diagnosed with cancer.

People understand actions more than words. When I left for India, his exact words were: "You owe me nothing; this is a reward for the work you have done, and the person you have been." Instead of making me feel obligated, he made me feel great that I had earned this privilege. At that moment, I realized that people always remember how you make them feel. During every major milestone, Steve always honored my contributions and never showed a lack of confidence in me. His genuine care and trust elevated our relationship, and my respect for him as a leader grew immensely. That respect translated into my making valuable contributions to the organization.

Credible leaders make a positive difference in people's lives. Those who lack credibility have a very different kind of impact, and it's dramatically illustrated in this story told to us by a young leader (who, understandably, prefers to remain anonymous) working in a multinational consulting firm. Her experience makes the same point as Kathy's and Shankar's, but from the opposite perspective. Here's how she describes a high-level senior executive who had a direct impact on her and on the lackluster quality of work and attitudes of the project team:

> This individual was very abrupt, short-tempered, highly emotional, impatient, and unable to communicate a clear goal to the team. This caused all the team leaders to dread having meetings with her and most team members avoided her as much as possible. Needless to say, it was very unpleasant and I spent a good portion of my time on the project wanting to resign.
>
> Considering the top four characteristics people expect from leaders—honest, forward-looking, inspiring, and competent—she only displayed competence. She had very high energy levels; however, she never inspired me in my role. Her intentions or goals

were seldom clear and her messages confusing. I also did not see her as honest. While I was assisting her with finalizing the project budgets for approval, we "adjusted" the figures multiple times but did not disclose this information to our client. It may be that she was looking out for the company, but I would not trust her.

This young leader realized, "Such a display of poor leadership has a direct negative impact on the followers in the organization." She also learned "about the characteristics that I admire and do not admire in a leader and this helped me identify those that I have, or need to become better at myself."

We've heard these kinds of stories over and over again in our research. We've heard how interactions with less-than-credible leaders have had a very negative impact. We've also heard how, as a result of interactions with their most admired leaders, people are made to feel more worthy, more energized, and more committed to achieving extraordinary results.

While leading a communications project team at Monsanto, Katherine Winkel had the opportunity to work with a leader she admired, and her description drove home the point that credible leaders produce positive results. She told us about her realization that "it was my own leader who had essentially enabled me to achieve my personal best as a leader." And Katherine reported another insight: "It's this very quality—the ability to bring out the best in the people around you—which makes a leader truly inspiring." Appreciating this relationship "motivates me to be a leader that helps others to achieve possibilities that perhaps they doubt are attainable."

Are you someone's "most admired" leader, or something else? How are you doing at helping others achieve possibilities they didn't even think possible? How are you doing at bringing out the best in others?

Credible Leaders Inspire Loyalty and Commitment

Irwin Federman, venture capitalist and former CFO and CEO, told our students at Santa Clara University: "You don't love someone because of who they are, you love them because of the way they make you feel." Irwin went on to explain,

> This axiom applies equally in a company setting. It may seem inappropriate to use words such as *love* and *affection* in relation to business. Conventional wisdom has it that management is not a popularity contest. . . . I contend, however, that all things being equal, we will work harder and more effectively for people we like. And we will like them in direct proportion to how they make us feel.[2]

Just how do the leaders who are liked and admired make people feel? We asked this question in our research, and you might want to ask yourself the same thing. In analyzing the themes expressed in over a thousand case examples, these ten words were used most frequently:

- Valued
- Motivated
- Enthusiastic
- Challenged
- Inspired
- Capable
- Supported
- Powerful
- Respected
- Proud

The rest of the words describing how people felt about admired leaders were similar. And they were all positive. Not one mention of *fearful* or *intimidated* or *stupid* or *sad*. Every case was about a leader who uplifted the person's spirits. Every story was one of enhanced self-worth. Every example was about how admired leaders strengthened the people around them and made others feel more important.

The conclusion is inescapable: when people work with leaders they admire and respect they feel better about themselves. Credible leaders raise self-esteem. They set people's spirits free and enable them to become more than they might have thought possible. Credible leaders make people feel that they too can make a difference in others' lives.

The case study evidence documents how admired leaders focus their time and attention on others. They do not place themselves at the center; they place others there. They do not seek the attention of others; they give their attention to others. They do not focus on satisfying their own aims and desires; they look for ways to respond to the needs and interests of their constituents. They are not self-centered; they are constituent-centered.

This qualitative data is supported by our quantitative research.[3] In our studies we ask people to think about the extent to which their immediate manager engages in credibility-enhancing behaviors, and then we correlate this with how they feel about their work environment.[4] The numbers support the stories. When people perceive their managers to have high credibility, they are significantly more likely to

- Be proud to tell others they are part of the organization
- Feel a strong sense of team spirit
- See their own personal values as consistent with those of the organization
- Feel attached and committed to the organization
- Feel a sense of ownership for the organization

But when people perceive their managers to have low credibility, they are significantly more likely to report that they

- Produce only if they are watched carefully
- Are motivated primarily by money
- Say good things about the organization publicly, but feel differently in private
- Would not be willing to stick around very long if the organization experienced problems

They are also significantly less likely to be proud of the organization, and they are more likely to see their own values as dissimilar to the organization's values, feel a weak sense of team spirit, and experience low levels of attachment, engagement, and ownership.

So does credibility make a difference? Well, if pride, team spirit, shared values, loyalty, and commitment matter, then credibility obviously makes a difference. But if managers are content to pay more money to increase productivity, to watch over people carefully, to know people are talking behind their backs, and to live with high rates of turnover, then credibility be damned!

The critical credibility difference is an increase in a person's willingness to put forth effort on behalf of the shared vision and values. Rather than acting sheepishly compliant in following orders, constituents act with moral commitment in following a common purpose. Rather than doing it because they have to, they do it because they want to, and because they know that what they do matters.

The credibility difference is critically important in this era of wrenching organizational change and global competition. Leaders around the world have pushed product quality and service quality improvement efforts to the top of their agendas. Every day new initiatives sprout up to fuel growth in emerging markets, generate gains in productivity, create a global information network, develop new technologies that empower consumers, shorten time-to-market, reduce organizational layers, improve service responsiveness, eliminate steps from the work process, shrink headcount, break the organization into smaller units, reduce the carbon footprint, be more environmentally sustainable, on-board a new generation of talent, and support a myriad of other programs.

But all of these are wasted efforts unless the people who have to implement the initiatives believe in the people leading them. It is the credibility of the leadership that determines whether people will volunteer a little more of their time, talent, energy, experience, intelligence, creativity, and support in order to achieve significant improvement levels. Managers can threaten people with the loss of jobs if they don't get with the program, but threats, power, and position do not earn commitment. They earn compliance. And compliance produces adequacy—not greatness. Only credibility earns commitment. And only commitment will get people to work beyond their job descriptions and to their fullest capacity so that businesses, communities, and economies can be greatly regenerated.

Sustaining Credibility Is a Person-to-Person Activity

Strengthening credibility begins with an understanding of the human dynamics of trust. Ask yourself this: Whom do you trust more: people you know or people you do not know? Your answer is likely to be "people I know." Admittedly, you may not trust some people you know well, but that is much less often the case. Much more often than not, you learn to trust those you get to know, or because you get to know them, you learn to trust them. Rarely do people view the folks they sit next to at work as not trustworthy. It is always the other folks out there, but not the ones they know.

Studies also show that people have more trust in members of their own work groups than they do in management, and that they are less cynical in dealing with their coworkers. Why? Researchers explain, "For one thing, it is simply harder to hold cynical stereotypes about people you work with every day. Research on prejudice also shows that people can hold stereotypes about general groups of others (say, management) but often modify or abandon them when dealing with individual members of the stereotyped group."[5]

Picture a group of factory workers sitting around a table analyzing their plant manager's leadership. At one point, a veteran employee says that if the former plant manager of the facility were to walk into the room, he wouldn't even know the guy. He then says that the plant manager they have now is the first ever to walk around and shake everybody's hand. Later, when the president of the local union is asked what he thinks of the current manager, he says, "She ain't got a phony bone in her body." We have shown this scene on video to thousands of workshop participants to illustrate the essence of how leaders earn credibility and how they lose it. One day, when we asked for reactions, one of the participants said, "That plant manager had to get awfully close for them to know her bones." Exactly.

The lesson for all leaders is this: earning credibility is a retail activity, a factory floor activity, a person-to-person activity. Credibility is gained in small quantities through physical presence. Leaders have to be physically present, they have to be visible, and they have to get close to their constituents to earn their respect and trust. Leaders who are inaccessible cannot possibly expect to be trusted just because they have a title. Credibility is earned via the physical acts of shaking a hand, leaning forward, stopping to listen, and being responsive. By sharing personal experiences, telling their own stories, and joining in dialogue, leaders become people and not just positions.

Too many leaders have become remote, out of touch, isolated, and insulated. People have come to see business, government, and labor

31

leaders as apart from them, not as part of them. A nation's capital is talked about as if it were on another planet, and corporate headquarters might as well be on a distant star. Leaders have not been close enough to get to know.

The secret to closing the credibility gap lies in a collective willingness to get closer, to become known, and to get to know others—as human beings, not as demographic categories, psychographic profiles, voting statistics, or employee numbers. By getting to know their constituents and by letting their constituents get to know them, leaders can strengthen their credibility.

What people want in a leader is someone who is honest and trustworthy, who is competent and has expertise, who has a vision of the future, and who is dynamic and inspiring. People are more cynical today in part because they believe their leaders do not live up to these standards. This gap is not likely to be closed until leaders are able to realign their own principles with those of the people they wish to lead. Admittedly, leadership credibility is not the cure for all the ills of cynicism, but by focusing on renewing their credibility, leaders can begin to narrow this gap and restore faith in the power of people to matter and make a critical difference.

And just how do leaders do that? How do they build and sustain credibility over time?

Doing What *We* Say: The Critical Difference

The answer to the question of how leaders build and sustain credibility is found in the responses people gave to the following questions asked in our research: How do you define credibility behaviorally? How do you know it when you see it? What is the behavioral evidence you use to judge whether or not a leader is believable?

The most common response to these questions was: *"They do what they say they will do."* Similar phrases used to define credibility included

"They practice what they preach."
"They walk the talk."
"Their actions are consistent with their words."
"They follow through on commitments."
"They keep their promises."

This straightforward definition leads to a simple prescription for strengthening personal credibility: "Do What You Say You Will Do"—or DWYSYWD for short.

DWYSYWD has two essential parts: one is "Say," and the other is "Do." Credibility is mostly about the consistency between words and deeds. People listen to the words and look at the deeds. Then they measure the congruence. A judgment of "credible" is handed down when the two are consonant.

In the domain of leadership, however, DWYSYWD is necessary but not sufficient. When you do what you say, it may make *you* a credible person, but it may not necessarily make you a credible leader. Why? Because leaders don't just represent themselves; they also represent other people. When leaders speak and act, observers assume those leaders are speaking and acting on behalf of their groups. Leaders must act in ways that are consistent not only with their own personal values but also with the core values that everyone in the organization stands for and believes in. Leadership is not about what the leader wants. It's about the needs and interests, goals and aspirations, values and visions, and hopes and dreams of all those who are represented. Therefore, to earn and strengthen credibility in the context of an organization, leaders must "Do What *We* Say *We* Will Do"—DWWSWWD.

That *We* is crucial to leadership credibility. Certainly as a leader, you are expected to do what you say. You are expected to keep your promises and follow through on your commitments. As a leader representing others, what you say must also be aligned with what we, the constituents, understand and believe. We are not likely to do what you say if what you say is not consistent with what we want. Leaders and constituents must be on the same path. The aims and aspirations of leaders and constituents must be congruent.

Forgetting the *We* has derailed many managers.[6] Their actions may have been consistent, but only with their own wishes and not with those of the people they wanted to lead. Insensitivity to others is the most frequent cause of career derailment.[7] When managers are inconsiderate of others' points of view and resort to the use of power and position to command compliance and to get things done, they are not leading. They are dictating.

Strengthening the we-portion of leadership credibility has three phases: clarity, unity, and intensity. If we are going to do what we say we will do, then first we have to be *clear* about the message—about what we want to say. It's impossible to be consistent when we don't understand what the words are or what they mean. Second, we have to be *unified* around our intentions. We can't all be going off in different directions based upon our own personal points of view. We have to have consensus about what the words mean. We have to have a *shared* set of values and beliefs. Credible leaders find unity among the diverse interests, points of view, and beliefs of their constituents. Third, to do what we say as an organization, we have to *intensely commit* to actions that are consistent with the message. Once we are clear and in agreement, then we have to make sure we use the values and visions as guides in decision making and action. Collectively we all have to put our energies and resources behind making the promises real.

The Six Disciplines for Earning and Sustaining Credibility

Let's shift the focus from the overarching behaviors of credible leaders to the actions that leaders need to take, day in and day out, to earn and sustain credibility. To further understand the behavioral dimension of how admired leaders earn and sustain credibility, survey respondents and interviewees were asked to provide specific examples of what their most admired leaders did that made them want to follow. Just how did leaders earn trust and credibility? From our comprehensive analysis of the common themes in the cases and empirical data emerged the six disciplines of credibility. The process of building and sustaining credibility requires you to take the following steps:

1. Discover your self.
2. Appreciate constituents.
3. Affirm shared values.
4. Develop capacity.
5. Serve a purpose.
6. Sustain hope.

We selected the word *discipline* quite intentionally, in part because its root originates from a word meaning "to learn." Someone who follows a discipline is a learner. Discipline also implies hard work and commitment to a way of doing things. Earning and sustaining credibility is not a casual exercise. It requires adherence and devotion to a way of doing things that goes beyond mere acknowledgment of its importance.

Here is a brief look at these disciplines, which are the focus of the next six chapters.

Discover Your Self

The place to begin the enhancement of credibility is with an exploration of your inner territory. Who are you? What do you believe in? What do you stand for?

To be credible as a leader you must first clarify your own values, the principles that guide your decisions and actions and the standards by which you choose to live your life. Values guide how you feel, what you say, what you think, how you make choices, and how you act. Once clear about your own values, you can translate them into a set of guiding principles, a credo that you can communicate to the people you aspire to lead.

But a leadership philosophy isn't enough. You must have the competence to deliver on your promises. You must know what you are doing and have the experience and training to do it. You also must have the confidence that you can deliver. You must really believe that you have the will and the skill to persist in the face of adversity. So assess your competencies not only against your job description but also against the values and beliefs you espouse and against the initiatives you propose. Determine if they are sufficient to meet the demands of the situation. Test your self-confidence against the realities of the challenge. Seek the developmental experiences you need in order to improve your capacity to lead.

Appreciate Constituents

Understanding your own leadership philosophy and capacity is only the beginning. Leaders can't assume, just because they have a clearly articulated set of personal values, that those values are necessarily aligned with the values of their constituents. Leadership is a dialogue, not a monologue. It is a relationship, and strong relationships are built on mutual understanding. To be a leader, you must develop a deep understanding of the collective values and desires of your constituents. Constituents come to believe in their leaders—to see them as worthy of their trust—when they believe that the leaders have the constituents' best interests at heart. Leaders who are clearly only interested in their own agendas, their own advancement, and their own well-being will not be followed willingly. Reach out and attend to others. Be present with them, listen to them. Go out and talk to your constituents and find out what they value.

Understanding and appreciating constituents' needs and values is made more difficult in today's complex and distributed work environment. Credible leaders know that compassion for the struggles of others, for the diversity of cultures and beliefs, enriches everyone. So define your constituents broadly and seek a multiplicity of viewpoints. By forcing yourself to look at a wide range of possibilities, better decisions and more accurate results will be produced. You will be more adaptable as well as more resilient.

Affirm Shared Values

Credible leaders honor the diversity of their many constituencies. They also find a common ground of agreement on which everyone can stand. They bring people together and unite them into a common cause. They know that shared values make a difference and give everyone a common language for collaboration. Leaders show others how everyone's individual values and interests can be served by coming to consensus on a set of common values.

Inevitably, conflicts will arise between diverse constituencies. Shared values give everyone an internal compass that enables them to act independently and interdependently, responsibly and publicly. In a credible community, dilemmas are resolved based on principles, not positions; on problems, not personalities.

Credible leaders build a strong sense of community. They get people together in forums to talk about their values. Part of your job as leader is to find the common ground and build consensus around a core of shared values. Affirm these values passionately and speak enthusiastically on behalf of your community. And renew your community. Do not take it for granted or allow it to decay into anomie and normlessness.

Develop Capacity

People cannot contribute to the aims and aspirations of an organization if they do not know what to do, and they cannot contribute if they do not know how to do it. Strategic initiatives to build a "sustainable organization" or deliver "world-class service" can actually make people feel weak and incompetent if they do not have the skills and abilities to perform. Therefore, it is essential for leaders to continuously develop the capacity of their constituents to keep their commitments.

You must educate, educate, educate. Bring the values and purposes to life, whether in one-on-one sessions, in large group forums, on YouTube videos, on webcasts, in tweets and texts, or in conversations and in presentations. Ensure that educational opportunities exist for individuals to build their knowledge and skills. Provide the resources and other organizational supports that enable constituents to put their abilities to good use.

To strengthen your credibility as a leader, give people more discretion and keep them informed. Set them free to experiment and learn. But also foster a climate of personal responsibility. Stress that in this age of liberation, organizations will only become what all their constituents want them to become. Everyone takes initiative. No one waits.

Serve a Purpose

Leadership is a service. Leaders exist to serve a purpose for the people who have made it possible for them to lead—their constituents. They are servant leaders. Not self-serving leaders but other-serving leaders. The relationship of leader and constituent has been turned upside down.

Credible leaders know that it is through their visible actions that their true commitment is demonstrated. When leaders affirm the shared values of an organization they are also vowing that the promises will be kept consistently. They set the example by going first. They spend their time, the truest indicator of priorities, on core values. They hold themselves accountable to the same standards as everyone else, and when their leadership service is inadequate, they make amends for it, just as they would expect others to do.

When a key value is at stake or when someone's behavior is inconsistent with the stated values, leaders must step in and make decisions based on matters of principle. By taking a stand, leaders let others know that they are willing to put their personal careers or security on the line in service of the principles.

So show others what is important to you and the organization. Audit how you spend your time. Determine how well the proportions relate to the importance of the shared values. Establish new routines and systems that reinforce shared values, and, when necessary, take dramatic actions to confront critical inconsistencies. Take a stand based on principle.

Sustain Hope

Credible leaders keep hope alive. Remember that people want leaders who are inspiring, uplifting, and energetic. An upbeat attitude is always essential, and it's even more important in troubling times. During times of uncertainty people need more energy and enthusiasm, more inspiration and optimism from their leaders than in times of stability and growth. Optimists are proactive and behave in ways that promote health and combat illness. People with high hope have higher aspirations and higher levels of performance. Leaders foster the optimistic attitudes that lead to more challenging goals and achievements.

In times of challenge and difficulty, credible leaders are also available as a shoulder to lean on, as a support, and as a friend. They are compassionate, understanding how their constituents have suffered and willing to make sacrifices along with them. They draw on their own knowledge and experience to offer advice and counsel. They are there to tell the team that they can succeed, that they can do it, that they have the will and the way to make it to the top. And as necessary, credible leaders reassess the situation and are flexible in planning how to achieve shared goals and set a new course or a new target if things aren't working.

Sustaining hope means that leaders are personally there for the team in times of need. Credible leaders recognize and reward people for actions that are in line with shared aims and aspirations. Recognition reinforces the shared values, providing an opportunity to tell success stories and foster feelings of appreciation.

In the following chapters each of these disciplines, in turn, is further explained and examined. The starting point for every leadership journey is the inner quest to discover your core beliefs and capabilities. That inner exploration is the focus of the next chapter.

CREDIBILITY MAKES A DIFFERENCE
Key Ideas From Chapter Two

- Credible leaders make a positive difference in individuals' lives and in the workplace.

- Trust is the base on which credibility is built. To earn and sustain credibility, leaders have to get to know their constituents and let their constituents get to know them.

- DWYSYWD—"Do What You Say You Will Do"—is the behavioral definition of personal credibility.

- DWWSWWD—"Do What *We* Say *We* Will Do" is what distinguishes *leader* credibility from personal credibility. Leaders represent their organizations, not just themselves. Leaders' actions must be consistent with the shared values of their organizations.

- The process of building and sustaining credibility requires six disciplines: discover your self, appreciate constituents, affirm shared values, develop capacity, serve a purpose, and sustain hope.

CHAPTER THREE

Discover Your Self

" "I know who I was, who I am, and where I want to be," said Dan Kaplan, founder of Daniel Kaplan Associates and former president of Hertz Equipment Rental Corporation. "So in other words," he continued, "I know the level of commitment that I am prepared to make and why I am prepared to make that level of commitment personally. I know what it takes to achieve success for me. That success for me comes from paying a big price, putting a lot of work and a lot of sacrifice behind it."[1]

Dan's words reflect an ancient commandment that was carved over the entrance to the Delphic oracle of Apollo, the Greek god of the sun, prophecy, music, medicine, and poetry.[2] This message—*Know Thyself*—remains as true today as it was back then. All leaders must seek self-knowledge if they mean to establish and enhance their credibility. As Steve Dellaporta, product manager at the U.S. Department of Defense's Manpower Data Center, explained: "To be a good leader you need to know who you are, your values as a person and how best to use these values in every interaction. Without knowing who you are, you cannot lead with integrity."[3]

Leadership scholar Warren Bennis, in his study of how successful people learned to become leaders, noted that self-knowledge is an essential part of defining a leader's integrity. "To become a leader, then, you must become yourself; become the maker of your own life."[4] He observed that knowing yourself is "the most difficult task any of us faces. But until you truly know yourself, strengths and weaknesses, know what you want to do and why you want to do it, you cannot succeed in any but the most superficial sense of the word."[5]

Your ability to earn and sustain personal credibility depends first and foremost on how well you know yourself. It depends on how well you know your values and beliefs, your skills and deficiencies, what success means to you, and the level of commitment you are willing to make. The better you know yourself, the better sense you can make of the often incomprehensible and conflicting messages you receive daily. Do this, do that. Buy this, buy that. Support this, support that. Decide this, decide that. You need internal guidance to navigate the turmoil in today's highly uncertain environment.

Our research indicates that to genuinely know the level of commitment you are willing to make you must discover and develop three essential aspects of yourself: your credo, your competencies, and your confidence. Your *credo* is the set of values and beliefs that serves as a guide to your decisions and actions. Your *competencies* are the knowledge, skills, and abilities that you use to transform your words into action. And *confidence* is the will to make use of those skills.[6] To be credible, you need to have trust in your abilities to do what you believe, especially in uncertain and challenging situations. Your initial steps on your leadership development journey are ones that enable you to discover your credo, your competencies, and your confidence.

Clarify Your Personal Credo

In our continuing studies, we've asked thousands of people around the world to list the historical leaders they most admired—leaders they could imagine themselves following willingly if they were contemporaries. Here are just a few of the names: Susan B. Anthony, Mustafa Kemal Ataturk, Jesus Christ, Mahatma Gandhi, Martin Luther King Jr., Abraham Lincoln, Nelson Mandela, Golda Meir, Mohammed, Eleanor Roosevelt, Franklin D. Roosevelt, Helen Suzman, Mother Teresa, and Margaret Thatcher. The entire list is populated by people with strong beliefs about matters of principle. All were passionate about what was right and just. The message is clear: people are admired because of their unwavering commitment to principles, because they stand for something.

Constituents rightfully expect their leaders to have the courage of their convictions. They expect them to stand up for their beliefs. When leaders are clear about what they believe in, they can take strong stands and are much less likely to be swayed by every fad or opinion poll. Without core beliefs and with shifting positions, would-be leaders will be judged as inconsistent and will be derided for being "political" in their behavior. Which is precisely what Deloitte Consulting LLP's Darren Gest recognized in one of his clients, which caused, he said, the client's team to "both question her orders and lose faith in her as a leader." And, unfortunately, as Darren pointed out, "even if the manager is offering sound advice, the project team cannot confidently execute because they cannot trust her as a guide." His conclusion is true for all would-be leaders: "When managers find their own respective voice and set examples through their actions, the greater team can achieve shared values—a consistent set of values by which it can operate confidently." The first stage of your credibility journey, then, is to clarify your values. You can't do what you say if you don't know what you believe. You have to discover those fundamental beliefs that will guide your decisions and actions. You have to create a personal credo.

Let Your Values Be Your Guide

What does it mean to have values and beliefs? According to the late Milton Rokeach, one of the leading researchers and scholars in the field of human values, "A value is an enduring belief that a specific mode of conduct or end-state of existence is personally or socially preferable to an opposite or converse mode of conduct or end-state of existence."[7] Values inform individuals about what to do and what not to do. They are the guiding principles in people's lives with respect to the personal and social ends they desire—such as salvation or peace—and with respect to moral conduct and personal competence—such as honesty and imagination.

Values are directly relevant to credibility. To reiterate: to do what you say you will do—the *behavioral* definition of credibility—you must know what you want to do and how you want to behave. That's what your values help you to define.

Values are the standards that guide your conduct in a variety of settings and situations. Through them, you can take positions on issues, choose your policies, and evaluate your own and others' actions, beliefs, and attitudes.

When values are clear, you *know* what to do—you don't have to rely upon direction from someone in authority. By knowing what means and ends are most important, you can act independently—or at least you can recognize that you may have a conflict between your own values and the values of the organization or society. In either case, you are in more control of your own life than if the values are unclear

45

and hidden. Values, in this sense, are empowering. Clear values enable you to decide your own fate. And while you may have to suffer for your choices—as the lives of many on the list of historical leaders attest—at least you are making your own decisions. As uncertainty and volatility increase, the need for clear and abiding values increases dramatically. Values act like anchors in a storm. They keep you from being pulled away and torn apart by the violent winds of change. They are your first line of defense when facing heavy weather.

Values and value systems also serve as plans for resolving conflicts and making decisions. If you believe, for instance, that diversity enriches innovation and service, then you will know what to do when the quiet members in the group keep getting cut off in conversations by the more vocal members. If, on the other hand, you believe in the survival of the fittest, you would be unlikely to intervene.

It can be difficult to behave consistently with every one of your values all the time. For example, you may believe strongly in the values of customer responsiveness and responsibility to family. But when a customer request for a special order requires that you and your colleagues work more hours than normal, you are likely to be in conflict. If you work late and have to cancel a family engagement, you may be seen as insensitive to your loved ones. If you tell your colleagues you can't work late because you value the time with your family, you may be seen as unresponsive to the customer or to your team members. By being clear about personal values, and by being willing to articulate them, at least you can engage in a meaningful dialogue about priorities. This permits the exploration of options and guards against the development of resentments and regrets. It's not one specific incident that defines the importance you place on your values, it's how your choices are made over time.

Values also serve a motivational function. They keep you focused on why you are doing what you are doing and the ends toward which you are striving. Values are the banners that fly as you persist, struggle, and toil. Referring to them replenishes your energy. Through them you can answer the question, Is this worth the effort?[8]

There are literally hundreds of methods for clarifying your values.[9] Whatever technique you choose, they are all designed to elicit your responses to one very fundamental question: What are the core principles that guide my life? You can simply start by making a list of all the behaviors, attitudes, personal characteristics, and such that are important to you. Or you can write an essay about your beliefs.[10] Or you can write a memo to your colleagues at work. Whatever process you choose, the end result should be a clearly articulated set of principles that you can use to guide your decisions and actions.

At first, don't worry about putting your values into any particular order, but once you've got your initial collection, take the time to list them in order of priority. Of all the things that are important to you, which is preeminent? What is second, third, and so on? There will be times when you may have to choose not between right and wrong, but between two rights, so you'll need to know your hierarchy of values. And keep your list short. Five to seven is a good rule of thumb. It's tough to pay attention to more than that at any one time. At the end of the exercise, ask yourself: Would I be willing to fight to protect these values? To die for these values? To go to jail for these values? (Many people have fought and died for their values, so these are not trivial questions.) The final list you come up with expresses your core values.

Now go public. Engage in a dialogue with others about your values. Talk out loud about them. And when you do, others may ask: "Why is that important to you?" or "Can you clarify what you mean by that?" Having to explain your reasons for a value and its meaning to you can further deepen your understanding of what's important to you. It can also help others do the same.

Dialogue does not have to be about well-formed beliefs. It's often exhilarating and educational to explore values with constituents. Some consider it a waste of time to talk about ideas and values, as if business has nothing to do with them. We have found, however, that 65 percent of people would like to have more conversation about values at work.[11] The discourse can be enlightening and even joyful when the questions are provocative. For example, in their classic book on organizational values, William Scott and David Hart present a very challenging question: "What are the requisite conditions of a worthy life in modern organizations?"[12] Try discussing that question at your next staff meeting!

Evaluate Your Values

In one of our seminars participants were talking about leaders they admired when the vice president of a large petrochemical company challenged everyone with this question: "Was Charles Manson a leader?" In his opinion, Charles Manson fit the definition of a credible leader: he had loyal followers and strong beliefs about what was appropriate conduct. He was dynamic and spoke passionately about what he believed. Others at the seminar suggested additional notorious villains who might be added to the list—Adolf Hitler, Saddam Hussein, Josef Stalin, Pol Pot, Osama bin Laden. How would you have answered this question?

In responding to such questions, the role of values in leadership becomes most salient. Leadership is a process and a set of practices. As such, leadership is amoral. The process and practices admit no right or wrong. All processes can be used for good or evil. Nuclear science, biological science, social science—each can be used to heal or kill. Processes themselves are neither positive nor negative. People give processes their charge.

Leaders, however, are most decidedly moral or immoral. Manson may have been a skillful and successful practitioner of the art of leadership in the amoral sense of the term, but he was *not* a moral leader. Anyone who would do evil has no legitimacy as a leader. Such legitimacy is determined not by the leader but by the society that envelopes the leader and the leader's constituents. Manson and those like him who take others down paths that violate the shared and sacred values of the societies from which they come cannot be called credible moral leaders. Moreover, the aspirations of moral leadership are to make people free, independent, and capable of leading themselves rather than adhering to the commands of the leader. Moral leadership is about attending and adhering to principles rather than following a prince (dictator, demagogue, or head of a cult).

The true test of moral legitimacy, says leadership scholar James MacGregor Burns, is "grounded in conscious choice among real alternatives."[13] Any leaders who would impose their will upon others and allow them no choice are not morally legitimate. Observe if a leader engages in learning the true needs and values of constituents. If there is more telling than listening, it is likely that the leader is up to no good.

At first this perspective about moral legitimacy may seem contrary to the notion that credible leaders are characterized by taking stands based on clearly defined personal principles. It is not. What it says is that leaders must first decide what they stand for, realizing that ultimately the constituents will choose their leaders based on moral judgments. Leaders should bear this in mind—and constituents should be more willing to take a stand against those who would undermine these principles.

Dialogue and dissent are critical to the values clarification process. Why? In a significant piece of research on the subject of moral education, Lawrence Kohlberg (originator of the theory of stages of moral reasoning) and his colleagues looked at whether one could advance the ability of young people to think morally. They found

49

that they could. Three factors contributed to raising the level of moral reasoning. First, controversial dilemmas were posed and disagreement was encouraged. Second, the group was mixed in terms of their ability to reason morally: some people were less developed and others were more developed. Third, the teacher's behavior was critical, although surprisingly only a single teacher behavior differentiated "change" in students' moral reasoning from "no change." That essential behavior was the teacher's extensive use of Why? questions.[14] Similarly, in our own research we found that a manager's level of moral reasoning was higher following a discussion with others than if the manager did not consult others and resolved the dilemma alone.[15]

The lessons for leaders are clear. To create high morality in your organization, it is important to hold the right values. It is also important to challenge constituents to confront controversial dilemmas and to encourage disagreement. And it is important to refrain from resolving disputes by imposing the will of authority. If ethics, high purpose, and high performance are important goals, then asking Why? questions is a better strategy than giving answers. And if personally confronted with an ethical dilemma yourself, the best strategy is to seek counsel. When the issues are ethically challenging, even the most moral people reason better in consultation with others.

Acquire Competence

Just having the right messages, however, does not make a person credible; practicing them does. But before you can do the right things, you have to know how to do them.

Competence is one of the key elements of credibility. Unfortunately, it has not received adequate attention in discussions of leadership.[16] In stressing the relationship-building aspects of leadership, the competence-building parts have too often been overlooked. People must have the knowledge, skills, and abilities to perform their tasks and live up to their promises.

To commit to doing something that you have no capacity to do is either disingenuous or stupid. There is nothing courageous about boldly saying you will launch a new product or turn around a factory if you know you have neither the skills nor the resources to do it successfully. Leaders must be aware of the degree to which they actually have the capabilities to do what they say. And if they lack the necessary competence they must dedicate themselves to acquiring it, or, if time is short and the demand is immediate, find someone better for the job.

Acquiring competence enables one to be genuine. People who make unfounded statements about their ability to perform a task or achieve a goal, or about their possession of noble attributes or desirable material goods, are called *phonies* and *fakes*. People who actually possess the attributes or accomplish the results but don't feel compelled to boast about them are called *genuine*. They let their actions speak for themselves. Think about those you consider genuine. Chances are they never boast; they just do.

People do not voluntarily follow the direction of someone they believe is disingenuous, someone blindly unaware of personal limitations, or someone who is consciously lying to gain favor or influence. If people follow someone's direction only to discover later that they were influenced improperly or deliberately deceived, they will say they were misled. Misleadership is the inevitable result of swashbuckling overconfidence accompanied by lack of ability. Even if there was no intent to do them wrong, people feel deceived or wronged when they have been misled.

To lead and not mislead, you must have the knowledge, skills, and abilities to consistently exemplify the values you profess. And that takes constant attention to developing your competence. Take it from David Maister.

David Maister is a consultant. He's so good that he is a consultant to consultants. While on the faculty at the Harvard Business School, David published research that got the attention of major business organizations. He decided to step out on his own, and he says that "at the end of my first full year as a management consultant, at the age of 39, I decided to take stock."[17] His account books said he had done well. But David began to worry about his value to his clients.

He recalled that the health of a business is judged not only by the income statement but also by the balance sheet. So he asked himself what assets he had as a professional consultant. First he had his knowledge and skill, and then he had his client relationships.

David began to realize that these were interdependent. If he relied only upon what he already knew, then he would only acquire clients who needed what he knew at that time. That, he surmised, was a finite number. Worse yet, his existing clients had already been served by what he currently knew, so they were not likely to hire him again unless he learned more. Then it hit him. He hadn't learned anything new in his first year on his own, and so he had a problem despite his gratifying income level. David explained:

> By definition, the unsolicited phone calls requesting my services had been for things that I was already known for. Even though each client project was customized (to a degree) I found myself doing basically very similar work for a variety of clients. I had not added to my abilities. What was even more shocking (and depressing) was the realization that not only had I not grown my asset, but its value on the market was going down—rapidly. Left untended, knowledge and skill, like all assets, depreciate in value—surprisingly quickly.[18]

David also realized that the value of his clientele "was not to be measured by the number of clients, nor by their prestige, but by how deep the relationship was."[19] If he learned nothing new, then he would no longer be of use to his existing clients and would only be able to work with those he had never worked with before. For a consultant, this could be disastrous. By flying from client to client he was not building the deeper relationships with any of them that were so essential to success in consulting. And by having to fly from one to the other, eventually he would not have time to find that next one. David's conclusion:

> I learned that unless I actively worked at it, my career prospects would inevitably decline, even when (or perhaps especially when) I was making lots of money. Having a good current year financially was clearly a necessary condition for my success, but it was far from being a sufficient condition. Keeping my career moving forward, even staying level, was going to take conscious effort.[20]

David's reflections give testimony to the fact that if you want to be promoted, if you want to be hired, if you want to be followed, then you have to continuously acquire new knowledge and skills. You have to continuously ask yourself, How valuable am I to my colleagues at work, to my customers or clients, to my stakeholders, and to my colleagues in the organizations I support? Your value as a leader, and even as an individual contributor, is determined not only by your guiding beliefs but also by your ability to act on them. To strengthen credibility you must continuously improve your existing abilities and learn new ones. And that takes time and attention.

But competence alone does not determine the capacity to act on your values. You must also have the confidence that you can, in a given leadership situation, apply your skills and act on your beliefs. There is yet another important aspect of self-knowledge critical to leadership performance. It is perhaps the deepest belief of all—an honest trust and confidence in your own ability to cope with the specific leadership challenges that confront your organization.[21]

Believe You Can Do It

Self-confidence is not the same as competence. Knowing that you have competence and believing that in a given situation you can use that competence to achieve your goals are different mental sets. Cognitive psychologists refer to this as self-efficacy. As Stanford University psychologist Albert Bandura explained, "self-efficacy is concerned with people's beliefs in their capabilities to mobilize the motivation, cognitive resources, and the courses of action needed to exercise control over task demands."[22]

Researchers have found that beliefs about capabilities partly govern the level of a person's performance. They observe that "a capability is only as good as its execution. People often fail to perform optimally even though they know full well what to do and possess the requisite skills."[23] They fail to perform optimally because they doubt their ability to put those skills to use in a particular situation. It is not only competence, then, that determines execution and outcome. Belief in one's abilities counts.

Beliefs about your capabilities influence your motivation. They determine how much effort you are likely to exert and how long you will persevere when the task gets difficult. In addition, the greater the self-efficacy, the less stress and depression people feel in taxing and threatening situations. The greater the belief in their own capabilities, the higher the goals people set for themselves and the firmer they are in their commitment to them. Self-efficacy even has the power to influence career choices: "The more efficacious people judge themselves to be, the wider the range of career options they consider appropriate and the better they prepare themselves educationally for different occupational pursuits."[24]

From this research, you can see that self-beliefs of efficacy influence the leadership roles you might select. If you believe a particular leadership task is outside your control or will require more time and energy than you can muster, you are unlikely to pursue that task—even if you know that it is essential to your group's success. Belief in your own efficacy influences the level of challenge (and leadership) you will seek.[25]

Consider some of the outdoor initiatives typically used in leadership development programs. One frequently used activity requires people to walk across a beam six inches wide. When the beam is placed on the ground everyone confidently scampers across. No problem. But when asked to climb a rope ladder and then walk another six-inch beam that is twenty feet off the ground, people react quite differently. Some say, "No way!" "You've got to be kidding," say others. And then there are those who race across like squirrels.

The point of this exercise is not to see who is athletic, who is afraid of heights, or who is brave. The point is to illustrate that execution of a simple skill is often situational. People *can do* it in some situations, yet in other situations they may not believe they can mobilize the motivation, the cognitive resources, and the appropriate actions to control the demands of the task.

This is an especially important insight for leaders. If you do not believe that you can meet the challenges of a particular task, even when you have the requisite skills to do so, you have no business trying to lead a group under those circumstances. It is not a display of courage to lead people when you have low self-belief. It is foolhardy. You could experience disastrous consequences and, more significantly, so could your constituents.

Leaders need to understand their limitations as well as their strengths. Of course, leaders do not have to give in to their limitations; they do not have to accept them as permanent. In fact, there is no way anyone can overcome a doubt unless it is confronted and unless the competence and confidence are developed to handle a similar encounter in the future. But leaders must not experiment with constituents as subjects. They should have well-founded confidence in their skills before involving others.

Leaders should also recognize that it is an honorable act to get out of the way and let others lead when the leader cannot mobilize the motivation, the resources, and the actions to meet the demands of a challenging task. They should make it possible for someone else who has the values, the competence, and the self-confidence to step forward and lead. Such an "everyone-is-a-leader" culture is certainly more potent than an "only-managers-are-leaders" culture.

In addition to competence, then, confidence is critical to leadership credibility. There are at least four ways self-efficacy can be enhanced: mastery experiences, observing role models, social support and encouragement, and reinterpreting personal stress.[26]

Mastery

The first thing you can do to enhance your self-efficacy is to learn to do the task well. You must get the training and experiences that enable you to be effective. Mastery does not come in small doses. It cannot come from the usual two days of training and on to the next task. It requires training and practice, training and practice, and more training and practice.

Mastery does not come from learning to do the easy things superbly, however. It comes from learning to overcome the setbacks that occur in the process. Mastery comes from patience, persistence, and perseverance.

It also comes from recognizing that *you* are the one who caused the performance—not luck, or other people, or a mentor, or the weather. To gain a sense of mastery you need to truly believe that you can personally achieve high-performance results.

Modeling

The opportunity to watch others who have mastered a practice is extremely helpful to strengthening beliefs in self-effectiveness.[27] To believe in your own abilities to master a practice, you need to see that it can be done well.

But it is one thing to watch the CEO do something well and another to see someone in your own position do it well. To increase your own self-efficacy, find opportunities to watch others like yourself performing tasks well. It could be anyone about whom you might say, "Hey. She's just like me. If she can do it, I can do it." Or, "I know him. We used to work together. I didn't know he could do that. Well, if he can, I bet I can, too."

Support

Hearing from those you respect that you're doing well is always uplifting. Social persuasion, as it is called, helps you learn to believe in yourself. You need to hear words of encouragement if you're going to work harder to be successful. And the more task-specific the feedback the better. If you are not getting enough realistic encouragement, then you need to ask for it from someone you trust.

Support is also a matter of being in situations in which you are more likely to succeed than fail. While you should continuously challenge yourself to learn and grow, prematurely placing yourself or being placed in a situation with a high probability of failure will not add to your sense of self. Try to structure the conditions for success by gradually raising the level of difficulty and by surrounding yourself with supportive individuals.

Reinterpreting Stress

One day we watched a man bounce a soccer ball from foot to foot, foot to head, knee to knee. He even spun around several times and still kept the ball in the air. As we watched, he must have bounced it a hundred times before he missed and the ball hit the ground. Truly a master at work.

But when the ball dropped, he swore, kicked the ball hard, and stomped his foot. Learning to perform well can be frustrating, even for masters. It's hard work, and often very stressful. When under stress, the body sends out signals. Based on these cues—aches, pains, and strains—you infer how you're doing. You read the signals from physical exertion and determine your limits. To continue the task at hand, you have to find ways to modify your beliefs about your capabilities when you feel those stress signals.

You can do this by enhancing your physical stamina through exercise, by using relaxation techniques, or by reminding yourself that this is hard work and it is natural for you to feel tired or irritable. However you respond, it is important that you not interpret the psychological or physical stress as a lack of ability. Do not allow your body to convince your mind that you cannot master leadership.

Claremont University professor Mihaly Csikszentmihalyi's classic examination of optimal performance provides further clues about how to strengthen self-confidence.[28] Setting your own goals, he points out, is critical, because this focuses your attention by defining a course of action and suggesting the skills necessary to achieve those goals. People who experience optimal performance get totally engrossed by the activity. They are engaged in it, fascinated by it, preoccupied with it. They attend to the activity constantly; such intense attention avoids self-consciousness, which is the most common source of distraction. By setting goals, getting involved, and paying attention you get "in the flow" and learn to enjoy what you are doing even when the conditions may be less than ideal. You achieve a sense of personal control over the circumstances and are able to find joy in many little things.

These same principles will also assist others in increasing their self-confidence. Having mastered a performance yourself, you might volunteer to help others learn it as well. You might offer them words of encouragement and help them learn to interpret stress as a natural part of the learning process. Make sure that they feel ownership for their goals, are able to engage deeply, concentrate, and enjoy working on this activity.

Sum It Up as Character

Credo, competence, and confidence are the content of character. They are the substance of self, the subject matter that gives meaning to people. This is exactly what one young project manager related about his manager: "Had she found her voice and communicated her values she would have been better equipped to manage and lead others. More importantly, if she knew herself better she would have had more confidence to manage her team." His takeaway lesson from this experience was that "when we find our voice, I think we find our confidence—the confidence to express ideas, to choose a direction, and to authentically be ourselves."

Those who are clear about their values and beliefs have laid the cornerstones for a firm moral and ethical structure. People who have developed the skills to enact their beliefs possess the moral capacity to achieve good ends with good means. People who have faith in their abilities to execute effectively and consistently even under stress and challenge display moral fortitude. Moral structure, moral capacity, and moral fortitude combine to make a distinguished moral force in the world.[29]

The quest for character is a noble one, though often baffling, frustrating, puzzling. Just when you think you have grasped the nature of character, it evades you. But if you wish to be judged by the content of your character, you must decide what content you wish your character to hold.

Discovering your self is the first discipline of credibility. In the next chapter we'll examine the second discipline, appreciating constituents. To earn and sustain credibility it is necessary for leaders to actively attend to and understand the varied and often conflicting needs, interests, aims, and aspirations of their constituents. The process begins with discovering your self, and it continues as you do the same with others.

DISCOVER YOUR SELF
Key Ideas From Chapter Three

- The ability to earn and sustain personal credibility depends on how well individuals know themselves—their credo, competence, and confidence.

- Credible leaders are clear about the values and beliefs that guide their decisions and actions.

- Values serve as motivational forces in our lives and as standards for resolving conflicts.

- Moral leadership requires providing people with choices and alternatives instead of imposing the leader's will.

- Before leaders can do the right things, they have to know how to do them.

- Leaders bring a value-added competence and are not the genius in all things.

- Confidence in one's abilities, especially in uncertain and challenging situations, is critical to sustaining credibility.

- The content of your character is the sum of your credo, your competence, and your confidence.

CHAPTER FOUR

Appreciate Constituents

"I have learned that a good leader takes the time to break the ice and gets to know his or her team on a personal level," said Hilary Hall, "but a great leader goes one step further and learns about each person's values, how they build trust, and what is core to their motivation and drive. They then share the team's values, as well as their own, and align the team around a strong focal point for working together toward a shared goal."

Hilary described one highly diverse audit review team that she worked on at General Electric. The team consisted of professionals from around the world, including a German, two Americans, a Belarusian, and an Indian. Before they began their work, their manager had everyone complete a questionnaire covering topics such as where they grew up, their favorite food, hobbies, and so on. There were also questions that dug a little deeper: what type of work they liked and did not like, work styles, the role they usually played on teams, and what they respected in managers and their teammates. After they'd completed the questionnaires individually, their manager gathered everyone together as a group to share their responses.

At the time, Hilary thought of the exercise as a team ice-breaker, a chance for everyone to get to know one another and build a sense of camaraderie, especially since they came from different corners of the globe. "Why else would I need to know that Matt enjoys Mexican food?" she asked. But reflecting back on the experience, Hilary realized that the exercise was more than just an ice-breaker:

> Our manager appreciated our diversity and wanted to align
> the team around a common set of values—both personal and
> professional—and at the same time show the team what was
> important to him, too.
>
> This was especially imperative since our internal audit work
> was extremely deadline-oriented, often stressful, and required us to
> be at the work site for two weeks at a time. It was a demanding
> work environment and I believe our success as individual auditors
> was contingent on our success as a team, which began with mutual
> respect and trust.

Despite the taxing work conditions, Hilary said that this was one of the highest-performing teams she had ever been on. It was also "a fun work experience," she added, "since we genuinely got along and enjoyed working together." Furthermore, it was one of the few times that she could remember when she sincerely appreciated the feedback sessions with her manager; she reported really listening to and respecting his comments. Bottom line for Hilary:

> I think if we had not aligned ourselves around common values,
> the effectiveness of the team, as well as the manager's credibility,
> would have suffered. We could have easily lost touch with one
> another, working according to our own standards, resulting in
> poor commitment and lost motivation for our common work
> goals.

Hilary's manager exemplifies the way credible leaders understand and appreciate constituents' needs and values. Through careful listening and sensitivity to others you can recognize their needs and offer ways to fill them. People willingly follow your advice and recommendations only when they trust you have their best interests at heart. You must reach out and attend to all your constituents if you wish to be credible. Credibility, like quality and service, is determined by your constituents, so you have to be able to view yourself as your constituents do. This requires effort and possibly new skills, but a natural by-product of attending to other people is that they come to trust you—and you come to trust them.

Researchers have found that organizations with adaptive, performance-enhancing cultures outperform nonadaptive, unhealthy ones precisely because of their emphasis on attending to all of their constituencies—that is, their customers, stockholders, and employees. By contrast, in organizations with nonadaptive and unhealthy cultures, "most managers care mainly about themselves, their immediate work group, or some product (or technology) associated with that work group."[1] Related studies demonstrate that putting others' interests first, rather than your own objectives, is also critical to building customer loyalty.[2] Leaders who are clearly interested in their own agendas, their own advancement, and their own well-being will not be followed willingly.

The credibility-strengthening process begins with clarification of your personal values and beliefs, but only by being constituent-oriented can you ultimately become trustworthy. A firm credibility foundation can be established only when you truly understand and appreciate—even embrace—the aims and aspirations of your constituents. When you appreciate and pay attention to others, you send signals that they are important to you, and that their input and ideas are valued.

Shift Focus from Self to Others Through Values

With the growth of multinational corporations and global market-places, the importance of finding an alignment between personal and organizational values (or person-organization fit) has become ever more critical.[3] One senior executive told us: "It can no longer be the CEO telling people what to do. It has to be the values of the organization which guide people's actions, so that no matter where you are in the organization, or the world for that matter, you know what is expected of you and how to take initiative to get things done."

Values, however, are so deep-seated that no one ever actually sees the values themselves. What is seen are the ways in which values manifest themselves in opinions, attitudes, preferences, desires, fears, and actions. Values can be personal, professional, organizational, or societal. As discussed in Chapter Three, values provide the foundation for the purpose and goals of an enterprise. They silently give direction to the hundreds of decisions made at all levels of the organization every day. They are at the heart of the culture of an organization, as well as at the core of people's personality. Scholars have argued that when managers fail to take values into account—their own as well as those of others—they will be personally ineffective, and the same will be true at an organizational level.[4]

For several decades we have been involved in systematic studies, conducted in both the public and private sectors, about managers' values and the strategies for aligning personal and organizational values.[5] The majority of managers report that even more time needs to be spent these days in examining personal values, and nearly two-thirds say that greater attention should be paid to values in managing businesses. While most managers feel confident that they understand their organization's values, they are much less confident that they understand the values of those around them (that is, their managers, direct reports, and peers). It's problematic that as many as one-fourth of frontline managers report not feeling confident that they understand the values of their immediate managers.

When asked what it will take to improve the quality of life in the future, more and more managers over the past three decades are coming to believe that improvements will require a society with a cooperative value system rather than mechanisms and systems dominated by individualistic efforts. Few people envision a better future by simply letting the status quo continue. Greater appreciation is also reported for the importance of partnerships between the private and public sectors in meeting common objectives.

"Look out for number one" is not the slogan that comes to mind when managers think of their most important stakeholder. Greater attention, managers report, needs to be focused on others' needs in the organization, rather than being directed toward personal needs. The high-importance ratings given to employees and subordinates signal a growing recognition of how reciprocal the relationship is between those who are led and those who aspire to lead them. Today's managers place greater emphasis on understanding the needs of their work group members and supporting the efforts of others than did their counterparts in the past.

Big shifts are reported in the balance between work and home demands, with the nonwork side of managers' lives playing an increasingly important role. Ever-growing numbers of managers are willing to turn down a better job offer or promotion if it requires a significant change in lifestyle—relocation, for example. Where executives had previously reported career as providing them the most satisfaction in life in the 1990s (54 percent versus 38 percent for home), they are now reporting just the opposite—62 percent favoring home and only 22 percent favoring career.[6] People want to find a more even balance between the demands of their personal and organizational lives. These trends create ongoing challenges for aligning personal and organizational values.

Despite the massive changes of the past decades, these surveys make it clear that in the area of values there are some dependable constants. The importance of leading by example has not diminished, and the personal qualities admired most in others have not changed. What people are looking for from their work and leaders has also remained constant. They want a sense of meaning and shared purpose in their work that justifies a personal commitment. They want their own values to be aligned with those of their organization, and when they perceive that they have these things, they will reward their enterprises accordingly with higher levels of motivation, productivity, and commitment.

Furthermore, the latest studies reveal that those managers whose personal values are most highly congruent with those of their organization have the most positive feelings about their workplace in comparison with those whose personal values are less congruent. Those with strong "personal values congruency" express significantly more commitment to their organization, and they feel more personally successful and motivated than their weak-personal-values congruency counterparts. Likewise, the strong-congruence managers report significantly lower degrees of work stress and job anxiety than do those whose values are out of tune with their organizations' values. These findings are not affected by the respondents' gender, educational level, or functional discipline.[7]

Amid the changes and the consistencies, contemporary managers don't report less commitment to work than their predecessors, but they do seem determined to work differently. Noticeable differences include a desire for more self-expression and preference for more organizational cooperation.[8] You should recognize these values, needs, and aspirations—and the importance of attending to them. You also need to appreciate that your constituents now cover a wider spectrum than ever before. To meet corporate objectives as well as constituent needs, you must broaden your own sensitivities and perspectives.

Learn About Others and How Diversity Enriches Performance

Whether on the floor or in the boardroom, Wall Street or Main Street, the Champs Élysées or Tiananmen Square, the fact is that work takes place in a multinational economic climate. It's no longer possible to thrive in the business, government, or independent nonprofit sectors by being responsive only to the neighborhood, or even the world, as defined by a few. To be successful in a multinational economic system, leaders in all roles, at all levels, and in all walks of life must learn to appreciate the diversity of their constituents.

The reason is simple: diversity, individual and organizational, is enriching. Organizations and individuals with a strong appreciation of diversity are apt to be creative and innovative. Being forced to look at a wide range of possibilities results in better decisions and produces more accurate results. It fosters adaptability and resiliency. An organization that values diversity thereby enhances its capacity to adapt and renew itself in a swiftly changing world. Given the radically shifting business and social environments, it's imperative that organizations open themselves up to more diverse points of view.[9]

Diversity does make the leader's job more complex. With greater breadth of resources, talents, and energy come new challenges and alternatives. More reaching out is required. More compassion and understanding are demanded, as is the ability to recognize that sometimes competing values and interests are legitimate and important.

In today's multicultural world, differences must be recognized and acknowledged.[10] Overlooking real and relevant differences can not only harm people, it can also seriously damage their productivity.

What makes for good working relationships between people with differences in gender, age, and ethnic or racial background? Researchers suggest these four characteristics:[11]

- The relationships involve the whole person. That is, you don't arbitrarily separate business from pleasure but include and acknowledge one another's personal sides (such as family, interests, hopes, and dreams).
- In excellent working relationships, a sense of shared history is developed over time. This fosters a sense of durability, remembering that the relationship has weathered both good times and bad times.
- These relationships are collaborative rather than competitive. Each person has certain strengths that can be counted on and well-known weaknesses that have to be taken into account.
- There is a strong sense that each person values and affirms the other. Each party is the other's supporter and admirer.

These characteristics are not restricted to relations between disparate groups; they contribute to successful interpersonal relationships of any kind.

Being able to build relationships starts by learning how to understand and see things from another's perspective.[12] When marriages or friendships fall apart, people often say, "We didn't understand each other anymore" or "We didn't see things the same way." The same is true for strategic alliances and mergers that fail to reap the anticipated synergistic benefits. And it's true as well for executives. Studies from the Center for Creative Leadership, for example, reveal that successful executives derail in their careers most often because of insensitivity and inability to understand the perspectives of other people. They undervalue the contributions of others, making them feel inadequate. They listen poorly, act dictatorially, play favorites, and fail to give credit to others when it is due (or sometimes even share it). The net result over time is that these traits and attitudes catch up with them. When these managers really need the help of others around them, they are left to fend for themselves, ignored, isolated, and on occasion even purposely sabotaged.[13]

You must fully appreciate others to enable relationships to work and to stay on track. The greater the extent to which each party comprehends the other's perceptions, concerns, and values, the greater is their ability to work together. So where and how do you begin?

Begin Appreciation with Listening

As fundamental as it might seem, the best thing that you can do to show others you respect them and consider them worthwhile is to reach out, listen, and learn. Professors Suresh Srivastva and Frank Barrett of Case Western University underscored this point in their writings on executive integrity:

> [It is] not the content of the exchange that is central but the experience of being taken in and heard, which not only affirms the legitimacy of one's way of looking at the world but then allows one to begin letting go of some defensiveness because the experience of affirmation increases one's capacity to affirm others.[14]

This means that you must not simply articulate your own philosophy. You must also listen to the philosophies of others. Building trust begins by building a personal relationship through listening. This means listening everywhere and to everyone. It means regularly walking the halls and plant floors, meeting often with small groups below the managerial level, and hitting the road for frequent visits with employees, key suppliers, business partners, customers, and other key stakeholders. It may mean learning another language if that's what a large portion of your workforce or customer base speak.

And with the explosive growth of social media, it also means that every leader must have a strategy for using these new means of communication. Social technologies such as Facebook, Twitter, and LinkedIn, as well as the tools of web seminars and videoconferences, enable you to hear from many more people in far shorter periods of time than you could when you had to call a staff meeting, schedule a town hall, or travel across the country to meet with constituents in another location. The information is also more likely to be unfiltered and uncensored. Charlene Li, a leading expert on these technologies and author of *Open Leadership*, pointed out, "As your customers and employees become more adept at using social and other technologies, they will push you to be more open, urging you to let go in ways in which you may not be comfortable."[15] Social media technologies are tailor-made for openness, and Matthew Fraser and Roland Berger of INSEAD business school have noted, "Chief executive officers are finally looking more and more at how social networking tools can extend their brands, create corporate cultures based on listening and learning, and establish their leadership profiles. . . . Web tools like blogs can help corporate leaders enhance their credibility by communicating directly and having authentic conversations with key stakeholders."[16]

Keep in mind, however, that the emphasis in social media is on *social* and not on media. They are ways to enhance your interpersonal connection with your constituents and to shrink the distance between you and them. They are ways to improve dialogue and conversation, not simply more efficient ways to broadcast your point of view. When it comes to social media there is, Dan Mulhern (author of *Everyday Leadership*) told us, "a difference between thought leaders and action leaders."[17] Thought leaders, he said, can authentically build credibility from a distance. Most authors, including us, never meet the majority of their readers and are likely to never be seen or heard by them. The same is true for other subject matter experts like professors, researchers, and consultants. Action leaders—those in the field working every day to mobilize others to want to struggle for shared aspirations—cannot sustain credibility without making efforts to connect face-to-face.

Your constituents want to experience you in living color. They want to know firsthand who you are, how you feel, and whether you really care. They want to shake your hand, look you in the eye, hear you speak in person, have a chat with you in your office or on the sales floor. And because most of your constituents cannot come to you, you have to go to them. This is no mean feat when they may be halfway around the world. While there are many virtual and social media options that can shrink distance, when it comes to leading action there is no substitute for the strong ties that come from face-to-face contact with others.[18] New mobile devices are useful, but you also need to invest in a few airline tickets.

The point is simply this: listening strengthens credibility. Listening is far more effective than telling when it comes to getting people to believe in you. When you ask other people questions about their hopes, their fears, their beliefs, their triumphs, their setbacks, their family, their childhood, their career aspirations, and then you listen intently to their answers, you are building a bond with them. There may be language differences, cultural differences, religious differences, age differences, ethnic differences, and socioeconomic differences, but all of these are a lot easier to overcome when you create a shared history. Listening to other people's stories is among the most ancient and most lasting ways to strengthen relationships.

Once you start listening, you discover how little you really know about other people. And that's the beauty of it: listening helps you to realize how much more opportunity there is for learning. Appreciation is facilitated when you adopt a learning attitude. It enables you to keep your mind open to what other people can contribute to an enterprise. This perspective will serve you especially well when working with people from diverse backgrounds.

When you listen you may also find out that you need to reexamine old assumptions. If you are going to find common ground with people who have had different life experiences and hold different views, you may have to question some of your past decisions and actions. This may make you feel uncomfortable and cause you to worry about losing face or looking stupid. Taking in new information, information that is contrary to previous positions and statements you've made, increases your discomfort and can make you psychologically insecure. It's no wonder that appreciating other perspectives can seem difficult and awkward.

One way to make the process easier is to acknowledge that others know more about some things than you do, even if you are their supervisor. George Petley, who was general manager of Kewdale Structural Engineers in Western Australia, readily acknowledged others' competence. Kewdale employees, he said, "know how to do this stuff better than I do. Some people like pretending that they are king of the hill, big boss, throwing their weight around and all that, but me, I know that what these people can do if you let them is terrific." For George, they were all part of the same team, working together and learning from one another.

Stephen Dunne, a business solutions consultant at Verizon Business, further explained how trust is gained through listening and joint problem solving. "I learn the most from our problems and by working with others to resolve them," he told us. "I believe this attitude increases my credibility with our customers, because they know that while I might not have all the answers, I am tremendously responsive in making things work for them."

Steve related a story about how one of his former managers built credibility by admitting he needed to listen more to his work team.

> [This manager] told us he had been reviewing some paperwork recently and discovered that the recommendations we had given him some months back on an important project had been the right way to proceed. So, he said: "I think maybe you all have been trying to steer me in the right track. I need to acknowledge that: You were right and I should have listened more carefully at the time. Can we pull these files back out again, backtrack a little, and can you help me understand this approach better?"

What Steve remembered from this incident was not that his manager made a mistake, but how important it is to listen carefully to others, especially when you may not initially agree with them.

Finally, leaders demonstrate that they appreciate diverse points of view by asking for feedback.[19] Credibility, as we've repeatedly said, is behaviorally defined as doing what you say you will do. So, to make sure you are doing what you say, it's important to find out how you are doing. Soliciting feedback is the reciprocal side of showing appreciation. When you ask others for feedback, you are telling them, in effect, "I am placing my trust in you. I trust that you are going to provide me with important and useful information about me, and I value your opinions." Because you show trust in them, they are much more likely to show trust in you. When you listen to them, they are more likely to listen to you. For this to occur, however, informal and formal feedback opportunities need to be structured rather than left to happenstance.

But giving and receiving feedback isn't always comfortable. In fact, it's difficult for most leaders. In our research, the lowest-scoring item on the Leadership Practices Inventory (LPI) is "[He or she] asks for feedback on how [his or her] actions affect other people's performance."[20] Asking for feedback makes people feel exposed. No one likes to feel that way. Still, becoming a credible leader requires self-awareness, and sometimes that means you are going to have to make yourself vulnerable. The good news is, when you do this, people are going to be more inclined to trust you.

Promote Constructive Controversy

The more diverse organizations are, the more likely they are to experience conflict. It's only natural that people from varied backgrounds will not always see eye to eye. But rather than suppress dissent, the most credible leaders actively encourage it and demonstrate an appreciation of different points of view—at least the kind that are constructive.

When team members actively voice diverse positions, the group becomes more resilient. Members are more likely to see their part within the whole, and their satisfaction becomes less contingent on whether they agree with the decision and more on their willingness to commit because of their involvement in the process. With diversity comes balance and protection against polarization.

When thoughtful dissent is encouraged, the result is much more than a heightened sense of collegiality; better decisions are reached. As Indiana University psychology professors Janet Sniezek and Rebecca Henry reported, groups were generally more effective than individuals in making forecasts of sales and other financial data. In addition, the greater the initial disagreement among group members, the more accurate the results: "With more disagreement, people are forced to look at a wider range of possibilities."[21] Other studies have shown that groups apply greater degrees of ethical reasoning to difficult decisions than do the group members making these decisions all by themselves.[22] Open and sometimes heated discussion by group members brings out ideas and perspectives that some have ignored or perhaps not even considered in their initial consideration. In articulating their views, group members are encouraged to talk about their values and the principles involved in their decisions, and this elevates the discussion to higher levels of ethical reasoning—and ultimately to better decisions.

Leaders encourage dissent precisely because it forces clarification of assumptions and ideas. University of Southern California professor Warren Bennis, author of many leadership books, observed that "whatever momentary discomfort they experience as a result of being told from time to time that they are wrong is more than offset by the fact that reflective backtalk increases a leader's ability to make good decisions."[23] The best leaders know that they will benefit from honest and open feedback, and that their decisions will be better when they have considered multiple perspectives. They also know that many people are reluctant to "talk back to the boss" or to offer contrary points of view for fear of being seen as insubordinate. That's why they make it safe for others to express divergent opinions and to speak truth to power. They know that the quality of decisions improves immensely when they do.

One perhaps counterintuitive stream of research finds that appreciating diversity among constituents encourages both open discussion and productive conflict management.[24] In a series of laboratory and field studies, Lingnan University (Hong Kong) management professor Dean Tjosvold and his colleagues have shown how the open discussion of opposing positions promotes the elaboration of different viewpoints, the search for new information and ideas, and the integration of apparently opposing positions. "Constructive controversy," as Dean called it, copes with the biases of closed-mindedness and inadequate evaluation of new information. It simplifies the problem and militates against unwarranted confidence in initial positions. This process, in turn, aids in understanding both opposing points and the problem itself, fosters greater development of alternatives, and results in stronger commitment to high-quality solutions.[25]

Credible leaders model the constructive controversy process with their multiple constituencies. They explain their present position and ideas, presenting facts, information, and concepts that support their views and providing a logical structure linking these premises to their conclusions. But they don't stop at that point, assuming theirs is the best or only conclusion. Credible leaders invite others to elaborate their own perspectives, which are often quite different and incompatible with those of the leader. These opposing ideas and positions challenge and provoke people's thinking. Appreciating constituents allows constructive controversy to stimulate innovative thinking and encourages actively searching for new information. Curiosity is aroused. Original positions are reclarified and reformulated.

By paying attention to the arguments and viewpoints of others, especially those with backgrounds different from your own, you will find it easier to appreciate their perspective and remember the facts, arguments, and reasoning they used to support their (alternative) position—and this is typically a two-way street. This elaboration and search leave everyone much more open-minded and knowledgeable about the subject. People become less rigid and more capable of synthesizing and integrating different facts and ideas into new patterns and more responsive positions. Repeated exposure to diverse thinking and controversy fosters more sophisticated, proactive responses, as well as higher-level reasoning and cognitive development.[26] And how you handle controversy and difficult situations has much to do with the levels of trust that are engendered.

Engender Trust

The simple truth is that trusting other people encourages them to trust you, and distrusting others makes them more likely to distrust you.[27] Dawn Lindblom, for example, had only recently been appointed executive director for the Red Cross in eastern Washington when Gail McGovern, the new president and CEO of the Red Cross, began touring the nation, introducing herself to the organization's leaders in a series of regional meetings. At the meeting Dawn attended, this question was put to Gail point-blank: "Can we trust you?" Gail's response: "I can't answer that for you, but let me say that I trust each and every one of you." For Dawn, knowing that Gail was going first—that Gail would earn their trust by taking the first step and trusting them, trusting their commitment and competence—made all the difference in the world in putting her trust in this new leader.

Before people will be willing to follow a leader's vision or act on a leader's initiatives, they must trust their leader.[28] To be trusted, you have to extend yourself to your constituents by being available, by volunteering information, by sharing your personal experiences, and by making connections with their experiences and aspirations. You can help people trust you by the candor with which you talk about your actions. This is especially important when discussing conduct that might look to others as inconsistent or incompatible with a prior promise. To enhance a reputation as reliable, you need to deal honestly with problems before they happen. As long as the problem is not recurring, this builds confidence about your trustworthiness by demonstrating your initiative and by reassuring the other party that you care about the situation and are doing something about it.

Becoming trusted also requires reciprocity, a willingness on both sides to enter into dialogue and conversations. It takes time, because while trust may sometimes be forged in moments of great drama, it is more likely to be formed by many small, moment-to-moment encounters. The richness of the relationship between leaders and constituents, like the intensity of a good sauce, is formed by letting the various ingredients simmer together.

How then can you become trustworthy as a leader? How can you behave in ways that facilitate trust? Research has shown that certain key behaviors contribute to the perception of trustworthiness.[29] To ensure and enhance your reputation as trustworthy, take a few moments to examine your daily actions with these four questions in mind:

- *Is my behavior predictable or erratic?* If your behavior is confusing, indecisive, or inconsistent, others cannot depend upon you to behave in certain ways across similar situations. They cannot make reasonable hypotheses about how you might react under new or different circumstances. Some degree of predictability or consistency is required for people to believe and trust in you. Consistency means that the same personal values and organizational aims will influence what you say and do, that your preoccupation with quality or customer service, for example, will not give way to the shifting tides of fashion or politics.

- *Do I communicate clearly or carelessly?* Sometimes people make statements about their intentions, however tentative they may be in their own heads, without realizing that to others these same statements are viewed as promises. If you frequently make statements that you don't intend as commitments but that others might reasonably interpret as such, then they may well believe that you are unreliable and not trustworthy. If you are clear about what you mean, there is less chance that others will find your statements misleading.

- *Do I treat promises seriously or lightly?* The more seriously you treat your own commitments, the more seriously others will treat them;

if you take your promises lightly, others will also. Problems arise when people have different perceptions of the importance of both your word and the circumstances required to justify not keeping your promise. Further complications arise when people can't distinguish between wishes or vague promises on your part and those promises to which you are seriously committed.

• *Am I forthright and candid or deceptive and dishonest?* If you knowingly mislead or lie, for example, making a promise you never intended to keep, other people have good reason not to trust you. There is no such thing as a little bit of dishonesty. Discovering that someone has been dishonest casts doubt over everything that person says and does. By the way, honesty doesn't require full disclosure. It does, however, require a clear indication of areas about which full disclosure should not be expected and an explanation of why it is not appropriate. Still, greater disclosure between people generally makes for better working relationships and easier resolution of problems should they arise.

One of the most significant payoffs from building trust is that it promotes greater risk-taking and innovation. This is because tremendous energy is unleashed within constituents when they trust their leaders. They feel liberated, self-confident, and secure enough in their relationships to explore new territories and opportunities and to take on fresh challenges. This is exactly what Ana Aboitz learned when she was chosen because of her Six Sigma experience to lead a process improvement project at UnionBank of the Philippines. "At first, I felt a little anxious," Ana said.

> I had never worked with the chosen team members. I also knew
> nothing about the project that was assigned to me: improving
> the bank's statement rendition process....I had full responsibility
> for the project's success, and I did not know how to pass on this

sense of accountability to team members who did not report to me directly. I was afraid they would fail and that this would reflect on me.

Ana started by acknowledging to the team that she had little knowledge of the statement rendition process and recognizing that it was the team members who had the technical expertise. She proposed that her role be providing Six Sigma guidance and support for eliminating obstacles the team might encounter. Then she asked the team to follow suit: Each team member had a chance to identify project responsibilities where they felt they could add the most value based on their expertise or interests.

Given the opportunity to mold their role in the process, the members of the team became more engaged in the project. Right away they began to brainstorm out loud and interact more with each other. Some members of the team decided to take on assignments individually and others chose to work in partnership. Through it all Ana reinforced their roles as the technical experts on the project and made good her promise that the ideas they came up with would be implemented on the operations floor. "To build collaboration, you need to let go of responsibility and give others a chance to take it on," Ana said after the project came to a successful conclusion. "By entrusting others with responsibility you are letting them know you believe in them and that you have confidence they can achieve it."

As Ana and other credible leaders know, trust is the lubricant for individual and organizational change. The paradox is that people cannot take risks unless they feel safe, unless they feel secure that they will not be unfairly treated, embarrassed, harassed, harmed, or hurt because they choose to take some action. When people feel safe, their defensive mechanisms are not aroused because their self-esteem is not threatened. They become more open (and vulnerable) to outside influence and to learning.[30]

Research studies document the claim that the very viability of relationships, and organizational success, is based upon trust.[31] Indeed, studies show clearly that trust is a significant determinant of managerial problem-solving effectiveness.[32] For example, the more that senior executives are trusted, the more satisfied employees are with their level of participation in decision making. This finding holds true even on those occasions when one's actual level of participation is relatively low.[33] In organizations in which mutual trust does not exist, people are more cautious, less open, less satisfied, more distant, and more inclined to leave at the first available opportunity.

When you are trusted your actions will generate fewer disputes. If you don't deceive others, they will have less reason to get angry or deceive you in return. If you are reliable, and others know they can count on you, then your words and actions will have greater power to influence them. If you appreciate people and show that you take their interests to heart, they can trust you to lead them. People will be less suspicious and better able to deal with legitimate differences. In every respect, developing the trust of your diverse constituents is critical to your success and the success of your organization.

Weaving together the richly varied threads of your constituents' talents and aspirations requires effort from everyone, effort that can be undertaken wholeheartedly only when trust is mutual. When it is, as discussed in the next chapter, people can direct themselves toward shared values and common purpose. The results that can be achieved clearly justify the personal and collective effort and commitment required.

APPRECIATE CONSTITUENTS
Key Ideas From Chapter Four

- The more leaders and constituents comprehend each other's perceptions, concerns, and values, the greater their ability to work together.

- Credible leaders actively appreciate the diversity of their constituents.

- Appreciation begins with deeply listening to other people.

- Credible leaders ask for feedback.

- Promoting constructive controversy leads to better decisions and builds commitment.

- Credible leaders trust others to be trustworthy.

- Credible leaders demonstrate their trustworthiness by acting in the best interests of others.

CHAPTER FIVE

Affirm Shared Values

Once there was a village in Nigeria where the people made their living by farming. The village lay in a large green valley that was lined with palm trees and bushes. Surrounding the village were fields with crops of yams, cassava, corn, and other vegetables. Just beyond the fields was a deep river that the villagers called "Baba." The river was a friend and a provider for the people: the men used it for fishing, the women washed clothes on its banks, and the children played in its waters. But in the rainy season, the river overflowed and the people were fearful of its power. So, at a place where the river wound beyond the fields, they built a strong dam to hold back the water.

There was a man in the village named Modupe, which means "I am grateful." Modupe was a shy, quiet man whose wife had died and whose children were all married, so he had moved to the top of the mountain overlooking the valley and lived alone. There he had built a small hut and cleared a small piece of land to grow his vegetables. The people did not see Modupe often, but they loved and respected him because he had the gift of healing the sick and because he was one of them.

One year at harvest time, the rains were unusually heavy, but the crops had done well and there was much to do, so no one paid it any mind. As Modupe stood by his house on the mountain, he noticed that the river, swollen from the rains, was straining the dam. He knew that by the time he could run down to the village to warn the people of the flood, it would be too late and all would be lost. Even as Modupe watched, the wall of the dam began to break and water started to seep through.

Modupe thought of his friends in the village. Their crops, their homes, and their very lives were in danger if he did not find a way to warn them. Then an idea came to him: he rushed to his small hut and set it afire. When the people of the valley saw Modupe's house burning they said, "Our friend is in trouble. Let's sound the alarm and go up to help him." Then, according to custom, men, women, and children ran up the mountain to see what they could do. When they reached the top of the hill, they did not have time to ask what had happened—a loud crashing noise behind them made them turn and look down. Their houses, their temple, and their crops were being destroyed by the river, which had broken the dam and was flooding the valley.

The people began to cry and moan at their loss, but Modupe comforted them. "Don't worry," he said. "My crops are still here. We can share them while we build a new village." Then all the people began to sing and give thanks because they remembered that, in coming to help a friend, they had saved themselves.[1]

You never know when a crisis might arise in your community or organization, and when you will be called upon to exercise leadership. But when you are it's absolutely essential, especially in uncertain times, that you have, as Modupe did, a set of shared values to guide you and the confidence that others will respond positively to them. It's equally important that the other members of your organization or community share key values. Modupe knew what to do because he had internalized the village's values. So had his friends. This is why all leaders must build consensus around shared values. Everyone in the organization needs to understand the fundamental beliefs that direct decisions and actions and the principles that are used to resolve the inevitable conflicts that arise in business and in life. Credibility is not just a function of clear *personal* values. That's the starting place. But for leaders' organizations to have high credibility, all members must align with *shared* values. Leaders build commitment to those values, and they get people to see themselves as part of a larger whole—as part of a community in which survival and success depend on a common understanding of purpose and principles.

Use Shared Values to Make a Difference

Shared values are the foundation for building productive and genuine working relationships. While credible leaders honor the diversity of their many constituencies, they also stress their commonalities. Each and every member of the organization certainly has unique needs, and leaders attend to those, but to function as a unit, team members must have a strong sense of the values and norms that bind them together. For people to work together effectively, they must agree on a few fundamentals. They need some common core of understanding to build community.

Shared values are the internal compasses that enable people to act independently and interdependently. Shared values provide groups with a common reference for making decisions and taking action. They provide guidance in dealing with critical incidents. They inform people on the standards for treating each other, for responding to customers, and for negotiating with business partners. They serve as guidelines on the actions that get rewarded—and those that should be reprimanded. They give everyone a place to go when an ethical dilemma is nagging them. When people recognize that there are shared values, they have a common language with which they can collaborate.

When individual, group, and organizational values are in synch, tremendous energy is generated. Commitment, enthusiasm, and drive are intensified. People have a reason for caring about their work. Individuals are more effective (and satisfied) because they feel they are doing something meaningful. They experience less stress and tension.

Organizations greatly benefit from shared values. Employees are more motivated when they believe that their values and the organization's values are aligned. They are more creative and innovative because they become immersed in what they are doing. When people feel part of the same team the quality and accuracy of communication increase and the integrity of the decision-making process is enhanced.

For example, as we discussed in Chapter Four, managers who share their company's values, and who experience congruency between their personal values and those of their company, report significantly more positive attachment to their work and company than those who feel little alignment. Those who share the organization's values, not surprisingly, also find their management to have more credibility.[2] A host of researchers, in a variety of disciplines, have demonstrated empirically that shared values improve personal and organizational effectiveness.[3]

As more and more companies decentralize—pushing decisions out of corporate headquarters into divisions, from divisions into departments, and from one country to another—they have come to appreciate how values provide a framework for finding common ground, and for integrating and coordinating efforts and perspectives. While leaders must honor functional, technical, and cultural differences, they also need to be confident that there are some core beliefs that everyone will respect and respond to.

Find Common Ground

Leaders are challenged to achieve what the late John W. Gardner, leadership scholar, founder of Common Cause, and adviser to six U.S. presidents, called "wholeness incorporating diversity." In his commencement address to the centennial graduation class at Stanford University, he told graduates:

> [The goal is] not to achieve wholeness by suppressing diversity, nor to make wholeness impossible by enthroning diversity, but to preserve both. Each element in the diversity must be respected, but each must ask itself sincerely what it can contribute to the whole. I don't think it is venturing beyond the truth to say that "wholeness incorporating diversity" defines the transcendent task for our generation.[4]

One of the most common mistakes leaders make is to announce which values are most important and then expect people to follow. They go off on a cloistered retreat, talk only to each other, draw up a list of values, write them down, distribute them to everyone, and then expect people to obey. This approach may have worked in the old command-and-control hierarchies, in which managers told and sold values, but it doesn't work in today's more diverse organizations. Leaders now must cast the net widely to capture the broadest possible understanding of constituents' values. Then, having listened, leaders and their constituents must learn to speak with one voice.

Determining the key shared values is not a technical problem-solving exercise; it's a process in which all the parties must participate. The process itself is as important as the product, if not more so. Participation is vital, because people's perspectives change once they are involved. When people contribute their own ideas to any solution, they are much more likely to own the outcome. They accept ideas they might otherwise have rejected. This is even truer for something as dear as values. Developing shared values is more about asking people for their input than it is about telling them the answers.

Consider the experience at Ortho Biotech.[5] Early in the company's existence board members developed a mission statement that went beyond the usual language about stockholders, customers, and employees. After heated debate, they took the position that in order to attain market leadership they had to fully engage employees of all races, cultures, and genders. Board members then joined with the existing managing diversity task force to form the Culture Development Committee (CDC), which was charged with creating a process to involve all employees in putting the new vision into action. Andrea Zintz, who was vice president for human resources at that time, explained that they wanted to "involve all Ortho Biotech employees in building the kind of culture we most want for our company." They invited everyone to participate in a three-day workshop where employees were told that they could expect to be "actively involved in examining and challenging the vision statement," and that they "will participate in examining and defining the unwritten rules (norms) of the culture." Further, the invitation explained, "there will be an opportunity to learn and practice skills that will be useful in bringing about a work environment where everyone can take part in the success of our business."

The first day of the three-day experiential learning program was designed to enable people to feel safe with the process, with the other participants, and with management. It also focused on the skills of giving and receiving feedback and seeking and telling, skills the planners felt essential to collaboration and consensus building. Day two began with a historical perspective. Andrea Zintz, Dennis Longstreet (president), Rich Gatens (chief financial officer and CDC chair), and other key leaders told their personal stories about the CDC adventure. They then described the new company vision and asked participants to think about such issues as these:

- How does the Ortho Biotech vision fit with your personal vision, what you stand for?
- What do you like about the vision? What does it do for you? What concerns you?
- What's missing from the vision? And what would you like to change if you were to suggest a change in the vision?

After reflecting on these questions, participants formed groups of about fifteen people each to share responses—and to produce a report from the group. Then the groups reassembled into a kind of fishbowl or open forum setting. A representative of each small group took a chair in the middle of the large group, along with all the members of the CDC. Two extra chairs remained open so that any participant who wanted to could come in and have a say. Group members could also take their representative's place in the center group.

Each group offered the CDC its feedback. These intense forums got to the heart of core issues of operating in a diverse environment—issues of race, gender, and level. And they were packed with emotion, especially for those who had invested personal energy in creating the original statements of vision, norms, and behaviors. Andrea says about her leadership role, "I can't stress enough how hard it is for people who are leaders to hang in there. . . . You have to hang out a long time in the listening mode. . . . You earn your credibility with your constituents through really hearing them."

The unfinished business of day two was taken up at the start of day three. Affinity groups were created—small gatherings of people who had like issues and wanted to focus their attention on how current norms and behaviors did or did not address their key issues—for much of the day's work. These groups came up with changes and recommendations for improvements in the statements of norms and behaviors. Representatives of each affinity group were selected to be part of another meeting of the CDC at which a final vision statement would be crafted.

Why go through this time-consuming and difficult process? According to Andrea:

> Creating a company where everyone can contribute their best is important to our long-term success. It helps us attract and retain the best people in our industry, and when people feel good about where they work, they can perform their best. We often find ourselves working hard to meet short-term results. In contrast, the program is an investment in our long-term success.

Over the past decades more and more companies, and functional units within them, have designed innovative processes like this for involving their constituencies in finding common purpose and building a community of shared values. Research has consistently found that constituents, across a wide variety of industries and disciplines, from frontline employees to senior managers, want from their leaders a clear response to two questions. While they can be stated in a variety of different ways, they come down to this: Who are you? And where are we going?[6]

People want to know the values of those leading them, and they want to see the bigger picture. They want to know if there is a good fit between what they believe in and what their leaders and the organization stand for. And they want to know that what they are doing makes a difference. When leaders engage others in a dialogue about the shared values and visions of the organization, people can decide for themselves if they're in the right place.

Create a Trusting Community

Community is an apt metaphor for organizations. Seasoned Fortune 500 executive Jim Autry explained that the workplace has become an important neighborhood for today's mobile and distributed workforce:

> By invoking the metaphor of community, we imply that we in business are bound by a fellowship of endeavor in which we commit to mutual goals, in which we contribute to the best of our abilities, in which each contribution is recognized and credited, in which there is a forum for all voices to be heard, in which our success contributes to the success of the common enterprise and to the success of others, in which we can disagree and hold differing viewpoints without withdrawing from the community, in which we are free to express how we feel as well as what we think, in which our value to society is directly related to the quality of our commitment and effort, and in which we take care of each other.[7]

Creating a community requires promoting shared values and developing an appreciation for the value of working together and caring about one another. Unless people know what they have in common, they see no compelling purpose that justifies commitment to the community. Strong communities, and strong and vibrant organizations, only exist when people are willing to dedicate themselves to building something greater than themselves. Shared values provide the common ground on which everyone can build. And credibility is enhanced because all the parties—employees, customers, and other business partners—realize that they have each other's interests at heart.

Credible leaders recognize that the metaphor of community goes a lot further in unifying people than does the standard notion of hierarchy or chain of command. Community implies that everyone's interests will best be served when working toward a collective set of shared values and a common purpose. Self-interests at the expense of common interests are frowned upon in a committed community. Credible leaders energize people to take actions that support higher organizational purposes. They structure cooperative goals and point out how collaboration allows the team to make the most of its resources. They let people know that individuals will be rewarded to the extent that the team succeeds, and that the group as a whole will be held accountable for the results. Credible leaders establish strong expectations that employees will develop trusting work relationships.

The place to start building a trusting community is to open up the lines of communication. That's just what Olivia Lai did at Kimberly-Clarke. And in the process her team learned to appreciate that trust goes beyond the team; it also extends outside the organization to customers.

Olivia's department decided to help customers become more efficient in their purchase and rebate transactions—a common purpose that they both shared. It started with one customer, who generated multimillion dollar sales annually and had been buying from the department for over a decade. The department already had a channel director, who met with the customer every quarter to go over results and forecasts. He was the closest to the customer and served as the communications bridge between the two parties. But, according to Olivia, something was missing: "All these meetings and the relationship building were done at the director/VP level. What about those who were actually processing orders or the customer service representatives who were assigned directly to this customer? Managing the relationship on the front lines was equally important. As soon as I took on this new project, I set out to change things." So what did Olivia do?

> One of the simplest improvements was to put people on my end
> in touch with their equivalents on the customer end. In the past,

if a customer representative wanted to clarify an order or explain a new purchase process, these communications had to go through hoops to get a simple message across. I am an avid advocator of relationship building through direct communications. It's the best way to ensure communication lines are open and ensures that both parties are consistently on the same page because we're sharing information quickly and completely. A strong customer relationship fosters trust and confidence.

By connecting her team directly to their counterparts on the customer side, she not only eased the burden on the channel director, she gave her team a bigger responsibility—and people felt a stronger sense of commitment to the task. Said Olivia:

My team had great ideas on where and how to improve, but they hadn't had the chance to carry them out. Here was their chance to take action. They had a bigger stake in the project now and trusting them to do their job enabled my team to be even more proactive and successful. Trust can be a very powerful tool if you truly mean it.

Olivia wasn't entirely certain about how her team and customers would react to her building a stronger sense of community and affirming a shared value of cooperation, but the results were quick to come.

Suddenly, the idea fountain was spilling over, and we had to prioritize and choose between them because we didn't have the resources to implement them all. The team's productivity and enthusiasm shot up. The customer became more proactive. They were calling us—not to complain but to thank us and to discuss their ideas and feedback with us. We had created a partnership that allowed us to freely communicate back and forth. Gone were the days when all e-mail, calls, and ideas had to be funneled through the channel director (I know he is quite relieved to have less in his inbox and voicemail).

Everyone on my team appreciated the trust they were given to work more diligently and effectively with the customer. Likewise, the customer appreciated our efforts and worked even harder to help us earn more of their business—if you can imagine that! To be able to enable your own team to do something outside the box, but also to enable your customer's willingness to work with you, that's a win-win situation.

Creating win-win situations underscores the central role played by leaders in both advocating cooperation and building a sense of community. Leaders like Olivia who establish trusting relationships inspire greater commitment. Their credibility is enhanced because they emphasize common purpose, stress the importance of collaboration, and promote open communication. In contrast, competitive and independent leaders are seen as both obstructive and ineffective.[8] Highly competitive people are often not trusted because they are seen as acting in their own best interests and not in the interests of the group.

Advocate Cooperation and Reciprocation

Relationships characterized by cooperation and community have higher levels of productivity and resource sharing than competitive relationships. Cooperative goals, across a variety of situations, have been shown to create higher expectations of assistance, more actual assistance and greater support, more persuasion and less coercion, and more trusting and friendly attitudes in power relationships than competitive goals. Cooperative goals result in better progress on the job and more efficient use of resources than competitive or independent goals. Beyond that, they also strengthen confidence in future interactions. When there is community, leaders and constituents assist each other by sharing resources and expertise, integrate different points of view and ideas to solve problems, discuss issues to reach mutually satisfying agreements, show initiative, consult with others, and follow proper procedures.[9]

Yet despite the preponderance of evidence supporting cooperation—evidence from classrooms, offices, and factories—the benefits from competition continue to be overemphasized. Changing this emphasis is a difficult task, but critically necessary to do for several reasons. First, individual as well as organizational success generally depends on sharing resources efficiently; this sharing is nearly impossible when people feel they are working against one another. Second, competition generally does not promote excellence: trying to do well and trying to beat others are simply two different things.[10] However, leaders cannot make team members believe their goals are cooperative; team members must decide this for themselves.

How do you convince people that they are members of a cooperative team, part of a community, and in the process support shared values and a common purpose? To start, people must affirm that the team has beliefs and principles to which they all subscribe. They must perceive that there is a common purpose they are all striving to achieve—and that success depends upon them all reaching these goals.

Jade Lui was elated when she received a job offer to be a recruitment consultant with the Ambition Group in Hong Kong. At that juncture, she had been in sales for four years and had only the faintest idea of what a recruitment consultant did. She was rather anxious about this new venture, but team manager Jessica Ho made the transition smooth for Jade and laid out the foundation for her success at Ambition. "During my first weeks at Ambition," Jade told us, "I was particularly observant of the dynamics amongst my team: 'I need a finance manager from the retail sector . . . ' 'I need a tax manager with transfer pricing experience . . .' And the rest of the team would contribute ideas—be it names of candidates or companies where such candidates could be found." Jade went on to explain:

> This active sharing of information was exactly as Jessica had described in our first briefing, where she explained to me the idea of reciprocity and the benefit of team collaboration. In the highly competitive recruitment industry, speed to candidates is central to being successful. With every new assignment, Jessica encouraged her consultants to first leverage off team knowledge, rather than first spending time searching the database. Her goal was to have the team help each other succeed and appreciate the notion of joint effort. She reinforced this culture by having each consultant discuss candidates and share market information during weekly meetings, and openly acknowledged consultants who contributed to others' success.

As team manager, Jessica negated the fierce competition among consultants that is commonplace within the recruitment industry. Consultants frequently fight over quality candidates because their bonuses are largely determined by the amount billed to clients for successful assignments. Under Jessica's leadership, though, norms of sharing and reciprocity were ingrained within the team. Rather than encouraging team members to vie with each other for supremacy, Jessica redirected the team's competitive energy and motivated the members to collaborate to compete against rival firms working on the same assignments. This ultimately translated into the overall success of Ambition.

While Jade's experience was within an organization, Evan Gilstrap's experience as manager of Purchasing and Facilities at Volterra Semiconductor Corp. was between his organization and its partner in Singapore, JSI Logistics. When Evan asked JSI if there was anything Volterra could do differently that would save its people time, JSI requested that all shipment instructions be sent daily in a different file format. Evan explained:

> We had been sending JSI shipment instructions in PDF format, which meant they had to visually interpret all the instructions and they couldn't upload the PDF format into a systematic format to do their work. This made JSI's job much harder than it needed to be—and we had been doing this for almost ten years. In addition, it was an extra step for Volterra to convert our shipment files to PDF.

Volterra stopped converting the files to PDF and started giving JSI daily feeds in the format they requested. In addition, they gave JSI the report reader software required to open and print documents from Volterra's system. "JSI was so pleased about these changes," Evan said, "that they didn't even blink about absorbing the additional forty-five minutes of work a day. It truly was a win-win situation. The law of reciprocation was at work. I led by first finding out what we could do differently to help them before communicating about anything that I might need."

Leaders must enable employees to explore and understand their common agendas, just as Jessica and Evan did. Projects requiring the team as a whole to make a set of recommendations, develop and produce a new product, or solve a problem all enhance the alignment of individual and organizational actions. Further, when team members realize that the work requires them to coordinate their efforts, the task itself promotes cooperative behavior and a sense of community.

It's crucial to structure the work so that individuals must cooperate and to make certain that people recognize how their roles are interconnected. Leaders ensure that people discuss how their responsibilities complement each other and how no one individual or unit can be effective unless others do their jobs.

Despite what is shown on so-called reality TV shows, people are generally helpful. Several hundred research studies show that most people are genuinely interested in extending a hand to others.[11] The secret to achieving this helpfulness is making certain that people feel confident enough in themselves to ask for help and to be gracious when supporting others. When the fear of losing to someone else diminishes, the need to gain personal power also decreases. Power sharing replaces power struggles. Empowering people confirms their basic worth and encourages them to seek continuous improvement, which, in turn, provides a supportive and helpful environment.

Your actions as a leader are critical to finding common ground and creating community. However, they can be undermined if shared values are not also affirmed through collective institutional actions, most typically in everyday organizational policies, systems, and programs.

Reinforce Shared Values Through Organizational Systems

The ethic that shared values make a difference has to be part of the organization's living culture. People must understand and agree that this is "the way we do things around here." Values cannot be just personal; they have to be affirmed by all members of the team. The structures and systems must be in place to reinforce the team's sense that what we say we value, we do.

When systems and structures reinforce shared values, people come to identify themselves as being members of a team and set the expectation that everyone shares in the long-term benefits. Recognizing this interdependency—that no one works or can be successful all alone—creates a strong sense of obligation to assist and support others. This sense of connection and belonging among people creates a natural incentive to engage in cooperative behavior.

In high-performing organizations this cohesive, cooperative team-work begins even before the first day on the job. It starts with the recruitment and hiring process, carries through into orientation and on-boarding activities, and is evident in training and development opportunities as well as promotion decisions.

Recruiting and Hiring

An organization's recruitment and hiring programs are critical mechanisms for reinforcing and sustaining shared values. An organization needs to attract employees who already share at least some of its key values and whose needs are likely to be met by working there. It'd be nearly impossible to create a sense of community if employees each brought with them a different set of personal values. In identifying the best companies to work for, author Robert Levering, founder of the Great Place to Work Institute, noted that people don't just look for jobs but for workplaces whose cultures are aligned with their personal values. Further, he determined that the best firms were finding people who fit the company rather than a specific job.[12] His observation is evident in the practices of those companies that regularly make the list of the 100 Best Companies to Work For.[13] For example, at Google the hiring process begins with an application and a phone interview, and, if the applicant is invited, at least four in-person interviews with teams of people. In the interviews prospective Googlers are always asked to solve problems in real time or to offer their creative ideas on a variety of scenarios. Four interviews can often turn into a dozen and take months because Google makes hiring decisions by consensus. While this process isn't for everyone, it is a reflection of the philosophy at Google, which includes core principles such as "You can be serious without a suit," and "Great just isn't good enough."[14]

When work teams are responsible for hiring their own colleagues, the question of shared values, in terms of fitting in with the group's norms, is paramount. Understanding these values and expectations helps people screen themselves even before they sign up.

Orientation

Orientation or on-boarding programs play an important part in transmitting shared values. At Zappos, the online retailer, the orientation process includes the *Culture Book,* an annual publication that includes contributions from hundreds of employees, partners, and customers about what the Zappos culture means to them.[15] The *Culture Book* is now over 300 pages and contains verbatim statements from employees, as well as partners and selected customers, about their views on the ten core values of Zappos. Every prospective employee gets a copy as do vendors and even customers. The leaders at Zappos believe strongly that "our Brand, our Culture, and our Pipeline Team" are the company's only competitive advantage, and you can see that in the words of those who contribute to the *Culture Book.*[16] A *Culture Book* project might not be right for every organization, but it's illustrative of how serious strong-culture companies are about reinforcing their shared values from the moment employees sign on, and even before.

Consensus on shared values doesn't just happen. Leaders have to be intentional about continuously communicating and demonstrating the values. At NetApp—on the 100 Best Companies list every year since 2003—one of its most distinctive on-boarding programs is called TOAST (Training on All Special Things). Early in their tenure about

101

a hundred NetApp employees get together with the leadership team to hear from them about NetApp's unique culture and values as well as the company's business objectives. Senior executives are always present for TOAST because of their commitment to making sure that employees understand what makes the place special.

Training and Development

Shared values are further strengthened and reinforced in training and development programs. On their first day at Qualcomm—after being exposed to the business and its core values—new employees participate in an exercise called "The Spirit of Invention." They are tasked to build one of the company's newest products using LEGO blocks. In the fifteen-minute activity participants receive change orders and last-minute instructions, thus making the process a simulation of much of what goes on in the daily life at work. After the activity the new employees discuss how they performed and the role that the core values of the company played in how they did during the exercise.[17] According to Qualcomm, "Ongoing education is a defining element in Qualcomm's culture, reinforcing the belief that the overall capabilities of our organization increase as individual skills and knowledge improve."[18] It offers over 500 classes per year.

The values at DaVita, a leading provider of kidney care, are evident in all the ways in which the company educates its employees. The DaVita Academy is a forum where teammates (that's what they call employees at DaVita) come together to learn about themselves, the DaVita story, and the company mission, and to have fun. It's a far cry from any other program you've ever experienced. The singing and dancing "Red Shirts" (DaVita teammates who volunteer as helpers) who greet participants at registration are the first clue that the DaVita

Academy is not your ordinary training program. Chief Wisdom Officer Bill Shannon (who prefers to be called "Coach") kicks things off by talking about how the upbeat environment is important in uplifting spirits in an organization that deals with patients who are burdened by kidney disease. In another activity Doug Vlchek, SVP Wisdom Operations, who's better known as "Yoda," tells the DaVita story. He talks about the purpose of the company, and says to the DaVitans, "If someone asks you what you do, you can tell them, 'What you do for a living is give life.'"[19] There are activities to stress the importance of working together as teammates and as a community. DaVita Academy is an impressive illustration of how an organization designs training and development not only to teach skills but also to communicate and reinforce shared values.

Recognition and Promotions

The question of who gets recognized and promoted in the organization is another key determinant of whether or not people will believe that shared values make a difference. Effective leaders make certain that there is a clear link between what people are recognized and rewarded for and the organization's values and priorities. Recognition linked with shared values has been shown to be the most powerful strategy that companies can employ to retain their best people and achieve extraordinary results.[20] Consider that in the Gallup Organization's Survey of Workplace Engagement the key determinants are items like "Has the employee received recognition in the past week?" or "Does his or her supervisor seem to care about the employee as a person?" As CEO of Joie de Vivre Hospitality, Chip Conley invited each of the fifteen members of the executive committee (EC) to talk for a minute at weekly meetings about someone in the company who deserved recognition and why. And at the end of each story, an EC member from a different department volunteered to call, e-mail, or visit the employee in person to tell them what a great job they were doing.[21]

At Yum! Brands, the world's largest restaurant company in terms of chain outlets (with more than 37,000 of them in more than 110 countries), recognition is an integral part of the culture, and people take advantage of big and small things to celebrate. One of their "How We Win Together" principles is "We love celebrating the achievement of others and have lots of fun doing it!" The "Yum! Award," which is a set of chomping dentures with legs given to all those who "walk the talk" of leadership, is given out by Chairman and CEO David Novak. Every leader in the company puts his or her own stamp on recognition awards, such as the "Big Cheese" hat recognition at Pizza Hut, the "Warp Speed" award at KFC, "Sauce Packet" at Taco Bell, and the "Big Leap Award" at Yum! Restaurants International. These awards, although in a light-hearted way, link recognition with shared corporate values. [22]

One of the most important, visible, and closely watched recognition decisions is who gets ahead (promoted) in the organization (and who doesn't) and for what actions and behaviors. Promotion decisions made solely on the basis of technical competence and without regard to values run the risk of undermining commitment to shared values. Promotions should reflect the strength of employees' commitment to the organization's values, as well as of their technical competence, much as training should clarify an organization's values as well as build technical skills.

Netflix is a company that works very diligently to ensure that corporate values are represented in corporate practices, maintaining: "The *real* company values, as opposed to the nice-sounding values, are shown by who gets rewarded, promoted, or let go."[23] Consider how its leaders explain their value of "high performance." Like every company

Netflix sets out to hire the very best performers, but unlike many companies it acts on the belief that adequate performance deserves "a generous severance package." This allows them to "open a slot to try to find a star for that role." You see this operationalized in the "Keeper Test" that their managers use: "Which of my people, if they told me they were leaving in two months for a similar job at a peer company, would I fight hard to keep at Netflix?" Given their aspiration to have a workplace where every person at Netflix is "someone you respect and learn from," they are also explicit about not tolerating "brilliant jerks" because they believe that "the costs to teamwork are too high."

How leaders respond in tough times often sends even more powerful signals about their commitment to shared values. For example, one leader we talked to told us about a time when his company's numbers were lower than had originally been targeted. The company's CEO, he said, announced that in order to maintain margins some shared sacrifices would be necessary. At the next all-company meeting the CEO told the employees that there were two options: one was to do layoffs while keeping all other programs intact; the other option was to cancel the bonus plan for the first half of the year. The CEO then said that senior leadership had decided to go with the second option in order to avoid laying people off. In that same meeting the CEO announced that all VPs in the company were taking a 5 percent pay cut and that his own pay cut would be 10 percent.

The reaction of one frontline manager was typical: "On the one hand I was disappointed, but on the other hand I felt like a valued member of the company because I was told about the options and the rationale for choosing one over the other." He went on to say, "Far too often in business decisions are made with no background and explanation to the employees." Said another, "Now I don't think the 5 percent or 10 percent drop in a large number has much of an impact; however, it was the thought behind it that was more important.

I felt that he reinforced the 'shared sacrifices' needed by taking the pay cut as he was asking us to sacrifice our bonuses." These kinds of gestures, even if they may have only a small impact on the financials, can have a huge impact on people's commitment to the organization and their willingness to accept the necessary sacrifices brought on by difficult times.

Leaders must be vigilant about ensuring that organizational systems communicate a consistent message about the espoused values of the organization. Affirming shared values and building a strong culture that reinforces the values (as evidenced in recruitment and hiring practices, orientation programs, training and development experiences, and promotion decisions) are not to be taken lightly. Recent research indicates that two-thirds of all employees see organizational culture as important to the success of their organization, and among younger employees nearly three-quarters think that's the case.[24]

Reconcile Values Dilemmas

Differences and obstacles are often found along the road toward wholeness and alignment of personal and organizational values. The first step in reconciling differences is for people each to explore their own inner territory, so that they are clear about their personal values and what they are seeking in a relationship. The second step requires understanding the other party's perspective and how that person sees the world from the other side of the table. All too often when people are unable to reconcile value differences, they blame the stalemate on the personality or the character of the other person. This is generally both ineffective and unfair. Behind every impasse usually lie some very good reasons—at least from the other person's vantage point.

Effective leaders appreciate differences and take them into consideration when building what Harvard University professor William Ury, in *Getting Past No*, called "a golden bridge." This bridge makes it easier for people to surmount what Will identifies as the four common obstacles to agreement: It's not my idea; This doesn't meet my needs; This may embarrass me; and You're asking too much, too fast (so it's easier to say no).

Instead of starting from where you are, pushing your ideas or values (which is the typical instinct), Will urges starting from where the other party is "in order to guide them toward an eventual agreement." This means actively involving other people in devising the solution so that it becomes their idea, not just yours. This requires discovering and then satisfying their unmet needs. It means helping them save face. (People all have a constituency or audience whose opinion they care about outside of the immediate situation.) It also means making the process of reconciliation and agreement as easy as possible.[25]

When values collide, a leader must confront and help people to resolve these dilemmas. As Charles Hampden-Turner, senior research associate at the Judge Business School at the University of Cambridge, warned, reconciling value dilemmas is not without risk:

> Confronting dilemmas is both dangerous and potentially rewarding. Opposing values "crucify" the psyche and threaten to disintegrate both leader and organization. Yet to resolve these same tensions enables the organization to create wealth and outperform competitors. If you duck the dilemma you also miss the resolution. There is no cheap grace.[26]

The process of resolving dilemmas is aptly framed by the word *reconciliation* because it literally means to "unite again." Scholars at the Harvard Negotiation Project have proposed the need to be "unconditionally constructive" in the process of reconciliation and getting people together.[27] This requires adopting a strategy in which both parties improve their ability to work together and advance their substantive interests, regardless of whether the other party responds as they would like. It means that the guidelines are good for both parties: they are, in fact, as good for the other person as they are for you.

One possible resolution strategy when values or principles conflict is to find a higher-order value or a new interdependency. The product and service quality movements, for example, were higher-order resolutions of a possible values dilemma between timeliness and quality, and between cost and customer satisfaction. By talking about total quality and involving the entire system and its processes, organizations found that they could increase speed, improve collaboration, reduce waste and cost, raise margins, and strengthen customer loyalty. The principle of "total quality" helped move the dispute from an "us versus them" mentality to one of "we are in this together." Sustainability is another higher-order value that brings together concerns of improving the quality of the natural environment with innovation and cost-effectiveness.

But you cannot assume that all values dilemmas will be resolved to favor previously prescribed shared values. Not all common values will be appropriate for all time. New values emerge and other values ascend as the world changes. Witness the rise of corporate social responsibility, sustainability, workplace diversity, distributed work teams, zero carbon footprints, affordable health care, ethically produced products, on-shoring versus off-shoring, and biodiversity. Wise and credible leaders build in processes that enable communities to renew themselves.

Renewing community and commitment to shared values and common purpose can make a strategic contribution to a company's success and adaptation over time. They are essential processes if you are to keep from being blinded by rigid adherence to a set of principles that no longer make sense. You can stave off decay and keep your community vibrant by continually cultivating and renewing the capabilities of the people in the community.

Effective leaders realize that shared values do not necessarily mean shared skills. Just as with the individual leaders described in Chapter Three, before a group can live up to its values, group members must have the competence and confidence to execute those values. If your organization does not have the skills, resources, and supportive climate to enact its espoused values, it won't be able to build or sustain credibility. It won't be able to do what it says. Education, training, and coaching are essential in building the competence and the confidence of team members. The next chapter explores how leaders develop capacity within the community and among their constituents.

AFFIRM SHARED VALUES
Key Ideas From Chapter Five

- To gain and sustain leadership credibility, leaders build consensus and commitment around shared values.

- Credible leaders enable people to see themselves as part of a community in which survival and success depend on a shared understanding of and commitment to common purpose and principles.

- Shared values are the foundation for building productive and genuine working relationships.

- Credible leaders create a cooperative community in which people appreciate that everyone's interests are best served by working together.

- Shared values can only be sustained through reinforcements built into everyday organizational policies, systems, and programs.

- Credible leaders confront and help people resolve inevitable values dilemmas.

CHAPTER SIX

Develop Capacity

Niki Mirisch, a talent agent at the William Morris Endeavor Agency in Beverly Hills, represented actors, directors, producers, and writers in the entertainment business. By the time Pranav Sharma became her assistant, just two years after graduating from USC, Niki had been negotiating actor deals for over a decade. Pranav described how Niki helped him develop capacity on the job:

> From the start, Niki created a relationship that allowed me to develop my competence and confidence. Rather than having me do remedial tasks as I had done for two years at another agency—answering phones, writing letters, submitting demo reels—Niki had me listen to her phone calls as she negotiated deals. At the end of each week, we discussed the questions I had about certain deals and she would ask me how I might handle such negotiations. She even shared with me her misgivings about difficult deals. These informal sessions fostered my self-confidence and made me feel involved.

Pranav recalled a situation when Niki was unavailable and for the first time he had to start the negotiations by himself. When he finally got hold of Niki and told her what he was doing, he said she had only one question for him: "Why hadn't you started negotiating the deal earlier? Handle it!" The effect on Pranav was eye-opening:

> Her tone in those two words, "handle it," made me realize that she trusted me. She believed I could handle this deal on my own, but I also knew that I was the one responsible if the deal went sour. I realized that we could not succeed without each other. We were interdependently linked. I finished out the negotiations with the producers and relayed the deal to her. Niki made me feel even more powerful when she asked me to get on the phone with her when she told the client the specifics of the deal. At the end of the call, she gave me the credit for making a good deal.

As Niki clearly understood, *people can't do what they say if they don't know how.* And they can't do what they say if they don't have the competence to execute. They can't do what they say if they don't have the confidence in themselves to try. They can't do what they say if they don't get feedback about how they're doing. They can't do what they say if they don't have any choices about what to do. They can't do what they say if the climate's not there to learn.

Credible leaders know that they have to continuously develop the capacity of their constituents to put shared values into practice. When individuals, teams, departments, and organizations grow more able to perform their jobs and keep their promises, not only are their reputations enhanced, the leader's credibility also grows. As a leader, in order to grow your own asset base, you have to invest in others. That's exactly the conclusion from the Hay Group, which helps *Fortune* magazine determine its annual ranking of the World's Most Admired Companies: "The industry champs that really did come through the recession on top differ from the stragglers in at least one way: They actually believe what every company proclaims about people being their most important asset."[1] By significant margins the three most admired companies in each industry were much less likely to have laid people off, stopped hiring, or frozen pay than their counterparts, and at the same time invested considerably more in people development. Champion firms "focus particularly on making sure employees feel engaged by their work."[2]

Leaders must provide the resources and other organizational supports that enable constituents to put their abilities to constructive use. In today's complex, connected, always-on organizational world, this means going beyond traditional definitions of jobs and even functional classifications. It means increasing the scope of work for everyone, especially those on the front lines. Developing capacity requires you to ask yourself about the assumptions you make regarding the abilities of the people you lead. Just how far are you willing to go to develop the skills people need to be able to contribute effectively to making shared values a way of life? You have to be willing to liberate the leader in everyone and distribute leadership across the organization in order to make yours one of the best places to work.

Five essential components go into developing capacity so that everyone can act in a free and responsible way:

- Competence
  People must have the knowledge and skill to DWWSWWD.
- Choice
  They must have the latitude to make choices based on what they believe should be done.
- Confidence
  They must believe they can do it.
- Climate
  They need a culture that encourages some risk-taking and experimentation, accepting mistakes as a chance to learn from experience.

113

- Communication
  They must be constantly informed about what is going on in order to keep up to date.

Fostering and sustaining liberated people is vital to an organization's ability to maintain its credibility. The only sustainable competitive advantage any business has is its credible reputation and the ability to deliver what it's promised.[3]

Build Competence: Educate, Educate, Educate

When Banic Fung took over a new team at UTStarcom, he found the technical background and capability of his team members needed to be improved. He wrote lots of lesson plans for technical training, and he spent time coaching his people after work hours. As he said, "I wanted to equip my team members with more technical knowledge in order to develop their competencies and foster their confidence. As a leader, providing training is a good way to let your team members become more capable and more qualified. And when they get the respect from other teams, they will have more confidence and be proud to be a member of this team." With the additional training and individual attention, people felt they were an important part of the team and were ready to work harder and more productively. Another benefit, said Banic, is that when "they feel successful on the job, they increase their understanding of and alignment with company visions and values."[4]

Credible leaders like Banic know that they have to invest in developing people's skills and competencies. In fact, the development of people continues to contribute more to productivity increases than technology or capital.[5] What's more, researchers have found that gains in economic confidence among U.S. employees are predominantly accounted for by those who reported that their development was encouraged at work.[6]

The importance of increasing competence is clearly visible in the 2010 Global Survey of executives conducted by McKinsey, the global consulting firm. "Building capabilities is a top priority for their companies: 58 percent of respondents say it's among their companies' top three priorities, and 90 percent place it among the top ten."[7]

In that same study, McKinsey reported, "Leadership skill is considered by the majority to be the capability that contributes most to performance."[8] But here's the rub: only a third say that their companies focus on it. Execution doesn't align with importance. For capacity building to have real credibility, it has to have more attention than that. The McKinsey study also offers another insight into how to increase the attention paid to development. In companies where the senior executives set the training agenda, training and skill-development programs are seen as more effective. The lesson: when senior management leaders walk the talk, others are more likely to follow.

The effects of encouraging the development of employees were clearly illustrated in Burak Ersan's experience when he was an intern at PricewaterhouseCoopers in Turkey. One of the department managers he reported to, Seda Erdem, took an interest in his background, what he was studying at Sabanci University (in Istanbul), and his willingness to learn business consulting even though his background was in engineering. One day, Seda came to Burak's desk, explained that they were preparing a proposal for one of Turkey's largest petroleum companies, and told him, "You and I will prepare a presentation together, learn about this company, figure out their ways, and determine the areas they may need help with." Then she handed Burak the company's annual reports for the past three years, and suggested that he go through them, look at their financials, select possible areas of improvement, and write a summary within a week. Seda told him, "I am sure you will have a lot of questions during the process, but you may come and ask me anything you want. If I am not available, ask the strategy team or other managers." For the following three days, Burak said:

> I consulted Seda and the rest of the team tens of times. Every time I went to visit her, she was tutoring me like a private teacher, pulling a chair over and explaining everything to me without getting exhausted or bored. Moreover, after her collaboration with me, I felt more integrated to the team and realized that my colleagues were also sharing more information and resources with me. I felt part of the consulting group there.

Burak said that he worked from home when he couldn't go to the office because of his classes, allocating his free time to the task and even getting advice from his professors at the university. After a week he reported his findings to Seda, and together they prepared a presentation to the client about areas of future collaboration. When Burak looked back on this experience, he realized how much Seda's leadership had meant:

> I was willing to make personal sacrifices on this project without anyone even asking me to because she believed in me and trusted me. By her willingness to teach and coach me, share information and give me feedback, my confidence was increased to the point that I could do this thing that I had never done before. Seda actually got much more from an "intern" than anyone else might have thought possible.

Leaders like Seda appreciate that they can bring forth greater efforts and accomplishments from others by trusting them. They take the time to educate their people, giving them the opportunity to exercise their judgment and offering them choices.

Offer Choices, Foster Ownership

Choice builds commitment. Choice produces ownership. Jack Stack, CEO of SRC Holdings, explained what ownership means for his constituents:

> We have a company filled with people who not only *are* owners, but who *think* and *act like* owners rather than employees. That's an important distinction. Getting people to think and act like owners goes far beyond giving them equity. Owners, *real owners*, don't have to be told what to do—they can figure it out for themselves. They have all the knowledge, understanding, and information they need to make a decision, and they have the motivation and the will to act fast. Ownership is not a set of legal rights. It's a state of mind.[9]

Credible leaders enhance this ownership mindset by making sure people have choices about what they do, especially in terms of how shared values are implemented. Researchers have written extensively about how choice is required if organizations and their employees are to provide exceptional customer service. They have observed that responsive service and extra employee efforts emerge when employees have *latitude*, or the necessary leeway to meet customer needs, and *discretion*, or sufficient authority to serve customer wants.[10]

Providing people with choice—discretion and latitude—liberates them. It gives them the freedom to use their training, their judgment, and their experience to do what is right. Without latitude and discretion, people cannot act on their own initiative, they cannot feel ownership, and they cannot make much of a difference. If people have no freedom of choice and can act only in ways prescribed by the organization, then how can they respond when the customer or another employee behaves in ways that are not in the script? Choice is central to feeling ownership and expanding people's capacity to act on the values that are espoused.

Pierfrancesco Ronzi told us how his manager at McKinsey & Company knew exactly how to apply these ideas. "He gave me the possibility, since the very beginning," Pier said, "to take on an important part of the project that involved high responsibilities and constant interaction with the first-line management of the bank." Pier went on to explain how his manager influenced his performance at McKinsey:

> First of all his giving me an important part of the project made me feel unique and fostered my willingness to give my best in this project; not only didn't I want to disappoint him, but I wanted him to be proud of his decision to trust me. And he was also really effective in letting me make my choices and sometimes my own mistakes. This enhanced my conviction that even though he was observing me, I had full power on my duties. One more effective thing he did was to recognize me and my achievements in front of other people. This made me feel important and strengthened my desire to run the extra mile.

Developing others' competence through choice and ownership does more than build the skills necessary to do the job. It also has the effect of increasing people's confidence to go above and beyond expectations.

Foster Confidence

People need to feel that they are in control of their own lives. They have a powerful innate need for personal autonomy and self-determination.[11] All people want to believe that they can influence other people and influence life's events. It gives them a sense of order and stability in their own lives. In fact, you can't lead until you feel you can adequately cope with the events, situations, and people that you confront. That's why credible leaders do everything they can to bolster people's self-efficacy, their internal sense of personal effectiveness, and to foster greater self-confidence in others. Credible leaders take actions and create conditions that strengthen everyone's self-esteem and internal sense of effectiveness.

Pier Ronzi was able to find that belief when working with the manager discussed earlier.

> I gained a lot of self-confidence that I was then able to transfer in the coming years both to my professional and personal life. He showed me the mountain, came along with me for the first part, helping me to find the best way, letting me go ahead but holding me when I was falling, then finally convincing me that I was able to go by myself, and I reached the top.

That manager's attitude and behaviors helped Pier to develop a strong self-confidence, illustrating the point about how effective leaders turn their constituents into leaders. Pier even characterized his experience with that particular leader as "a lesson on how to enable other people to act." He continued, "His example activated a positive loop that led me to think that I can also take these same actions with others; that's what I've tried to do after this experience."

Pier's conclusion is borne out by the research. In a classic series of innovative experiments, Stanford University professor Albert Bandura and University of Western Australia professor Robert Wood documented that self-confidence affects people's performance. In one study, managers were told that decision making was a skill developed through practice: the more one worked at it, the more capable one became. Other managers were told that decision making reflected their basic intellectual aptitude—the higher their underlying cognitive capacities, the better their decision-making ability. Working with a simulated organization, both groups of managers dealt with a series of production orders, requiring various staffing decisions and establishing different performance

119

targets. Managers who believed that decision making was a skill that could be acquired set challenging goals for themselves, even in the face of difficult performance standards; they used good problem-solving strategies and fostered organizational productivity. Their counterparts, who didn't believe they had the necessary decision-making ability, lost confidence in themselves as they encountered difficulties. They lowered their aspirations for the organization; their problem solving deteriorated, and organizational productivity declined.[12]

Another interesting finding from these studies was how the managers who lost confidence in their own judgments tended to find fault with their people. Indeed, they were quite uncharitable about their employees, regarding them as not capable of being motivated and unworthy of much supervisory effort. If given the option, the managers reported, they would have fired many of these employees.

In a related experiment, one group of managers was told that organizations and people are easily changeable or predictable. Another group was told, "Work habits of employees are not that easily changeable, even by good guidance. Small changes do not necessarily improve overall outcomes." Those managers with the confidence that they could influence organizational outcomes by their actions maintained a higher level of performance than those who felt they could do little to change things. The latter group lost faith in their capabilities. As their aspirations declined, so did organizational performance levels.[13]

What the research and Pier's experience illustrate is that believing in your ability to handle the job, no matter how difficult, is essential in promoting and sustaining consistent efforts. Fostering self-confidence is not a warmed-over version of the power of positive thinking. It's a powerful way to improve decision making and performance. By communicating to your constituents that you believe they will be successful, you help people to persevere in the face of difficult challenges.

While you may begin with words of encouragement, support, and praise, the most effective means of raising people's self-confidence is to provide actual experience. You need to give people an opportunity to perform successfully. Typically an initial success experience, followed by a series of small successes over a period of time, form the basis for enhancing people's sense of personal effectiveness. The leader's challenge is to create situations for small wins, structuring tasks in such a way that they can be broken down into doable pieces, with each success building up the person's sense of competence. Creating a climate where learning is stressed and people feel comfortable making mistakes is another important way to develop individual and organizational productivity.

Create a Climate for Learning

Developing capacity requires that leaders provide a climate conducive to learning. As discussed in Chapter Four, for people to be capable of learning they have to be in an environment in which they feel safe. Why the concern for safe surroundings? Because when people are learning, they never get it right the first time. Mistakes are inevitable. People need to know that failure while learning won't be punished. That means they have to trust the system and the people involved. A learning climate, characterized by trust and openness, is a critical precursor to any successful organizational change effort.[14]

With trust and openness comes greater willingness to communicate about feelings and about problems. As individuals are listened to, more information becomes available, and people experience greater common ground and perceive more reasons to engage in cooperative behavior. They feel less motivation to defend either themselves or the status quo, and are much more willing to take on challenging new assignments.

121

By its nature, the hugely creative public relations industry is always in need of fresh ideas and fortitude to take up new challenges. Jenny Chong had zero high-tech PR experience when she first joined the Los Angeles–based high-technology public relations agency Terpin Communications. Throughout her first month at the agency, everyone was overwhelmed with preparations for the annual Consumer Electronics Show. With limited exposure to the conference, as well as in the high-tech PR arena, Jenny told us, "I was hesitant to share my original viewpoints due to the anxiety of ruining this monumental event." However, she found that their manager had, in her words, "constructed an environment where everyone felt safe to make mistakes and empowered us to be innovative and assertive to draw our own conclusions." He had told her that part of his mission "is to turn you young folks into future leaders. How? To acknowledge and encourage you." On a personal level, Jenny felt the effects of that encouragement from the start:

> His unconditional trust and support boosted my confidence level and fostered knowledge exchange among teammates. When I failed to articulate my ideas during sales meetings due to low self-confidence, he trained me to be a more self-assured individual by taking me to more meetings so I could practice. He gradually gave over control to me as time went by.

As she and her colleagues were organizing the inaugural CES Media Party for their start-up clients, they were worried about the media turnout rate. With a one-month time line, they were responsible for preparing the media event in areas ranging from logistics and hospitality to media invitations and strategic planning. Yet, she says, their manager never limited their creativity even though they were short of prior CES experience.

> He proactively provided guidelines and inspired us on how we could maximize the performance on a personal and organizational

level. His enthusiasm and acknowledgment led to a strong sense of our ownership and responsibility to drive for the best. He also facilitated our working relationships by encouraging us to have regular team lunches to brainstorm ideas and share our distinctive past experiences. A sense of interdependence and collaboration was embedded in the team—where we relied on, respected, and valued each other. Everyone was highly involved in all the projects and willing to help even if it was something beyond their job scope.

What leaders like Jenny's understand is that people can't really be expected to learn and move out of their comfort zones if they aren't given the opportunity to make a mistake. In any new endeavor there is a learning curve: generally performance goes down before it goes up. Think about the last time you installed new software on your personal computer. The objective is always to improve your performance. Right? So, what happened to your productivity at the start? More than likely it went down before it could go up (and if it went up right from the start, then you were simply underperforming all along). You need to make it easy to learn from mistakes. You need to be concerned with maximizing learning, not minimizing mistakes.

For more than two decades Stanford psychology professor Carol Dweck has been researching mindsets. She's looked specifically at two types: the fixed mindset and the growth mindset. "The growth mindset," she says, "is based on the belief that your basic qualities are things you can cultivate through your efforts."[15] Individuals who have a growth mindset believe people can learn to be better leaders—that they are made and not born. She compares this to a *fixed mindset*—"believing that your qualities are carved in stone."[16] Those with the fixed mindset think leaders are born, and that no amount of training is going to make you any better than you naturally are.

In study after study Carol and her colleagues have found that those with a fixed mindset tend to look at any failure as an indication that they are not very competent, and they tend to avoid situations in which they might make mistakes or fail. They don't want to take on anything that would cause them to not do well. They don't take on difficult challenges that are beyond their current abilities. On the other hand, those with a growth mindset view failure as a learning opportunity, and they are more inclined to embrace risk and challenge. Leaders need to create a climate in which experimentation, risk, and learning are prized and rewarded—a climate that fosters a growth mindset.

Credible leaders are great learners, and they regard mistakes as learning opportunities, not the end of the world.[17] In fact, because they appreciate mistakes as an essential part of the learning process, these leaders develop capacity by helping others break out of old patterns of thinking. Mired down in a numbing daily routine, people often behave automatically, stop thinking for themselves, and form unquestioning attitudes, or mindsets, based upon the first information they hear.[18] Credible leaders encourage their constituents to question routines, challenge assumptions, and continually look at what is going on from changing perspectives.

How to create conditions for different mindsets was well illustrated in a classic psychological experiment. One group of people was shown a collection of familiar objects and told specifically what they were, for example, "This is a hair dryer," and "This is a dog's chew toy." Another group was shown the same objects but told conditionally, "This *could be* a hair dryer," and "This *could be* a dog's chew toy." Sometime later, the experimenters intentionally created a need for an eraser. Only the second group, those who had been conditionally introduced to the objects, thought the dog's chew toy could be used in this new way.[19] The intuitive understanding that a single thing is—or could be—many things, depending upon how you look at it, is central to the learning climate leaders create. Adopting a "could be" attitude, envisioning many possibilities and alternative scenarios, promotes creativity.[20] And creativity has risen to the top of the list of what leaders need in this highly complex world, according to a global study by IBM.[21] A majority of senior executives and students now see creativity as vital to economic recovery and to competing in the global economy. Creativity, experimentation, and innovation can only thrive where there's a climate for learning.

Share Information, Give Feedback

Sharing information is essential to developing people's capacity, and to building and sustaining credibility. When there's a high degree of transparency, and when information is easily available and accessible, people come to trust their leaders, their team members, and their organizations. When it's hard to get, kept on a "need to know" basis, and hidden from view people can more easily become suspicious and cynical.[22]

Cheryl Breetwor, for example, held open strategy sessions when she was president of ShareData. Rather than closeting a small group of key executives to develop a strategy based on her own agenda, she held a series of meetings over several days and allowed the larger group to develop and help choose alternatives. As a result of having all the information, everyone knew what needed to be accomplished and why. Plus, having been involved in developing the plan, people were committed to it; their ownership was increased.

Communication and feedback are central to what is going on at HCL Technologies, which sells business and information technology services (based in New Delhi, India, but with operations in twenty-six countries).[23] Not unlike SRC Holdings, mentioned earlier in the chapter, HCL focuses on making sure that everyone knows the rules of the game; that is, how the company makes money and generates cash. For example, detailed financial information, broken out by business unit, is delivered regularly to employee desktops. People can figure out for themselves whether or not they are contributing to the company's growth. This transparency has stimulated and opened up communications channels so that employees ask more questions, volunteer more ideas, and challenge the status quo more often by initiating innovative actions.

Similarly, all employee appraisals are posted on the company's intranet, and anyone at any level can give feedback on anybody else, including the CEO. And as the CEO, Vineet Nayar, explained: "Good or bad, we all learn from the results. It's open, it's transparent, and the impact is positive. We find that this practice is motivating people to change their behavior. They try harder."[24]

Leaders like Cheryl and Vineet understand that unless they communicate and share information with their constituents few will take much interest in what is going on. Unless people see and experience the effects of what they do, they won't care. When leaders share information rather than guard it, people recognize that they are included and respected. A greater two-way flow of information is opened. Sharing information also lets people know the reasons behind decisions, typically how they are linked to shared values and common purpose. When everyone has the same information, understands that he or she is part of a community, and shares common values and interests, the results come more easily. Everyone can sing in unison, off the same page of the same song sheet.

Chapter Five highlighted the significance of affirming shared values and common purpose. But commitment, as they've learned at HCL Technologies, cannot be sustained unless people know how they are doing. Research clearly indicates that individuals' motivation to increase their productivity on a task increases only when they have a challenging goal and receive feedback on their progress.[25]

With detailed feedback that includes such factors as quality, quantity, speed, timeliness, and customer service, people can become self-corrective and can more easily understand their interconnectedness with the big picture.[26] With feedback they can determine what help they need from others and also who might be able to benefit from their assistance.

What happens when feedback shows that performance has fallen short of aspirations? Won't this information be discouraging? It all depends on people's beliefs in their capabilities. People who doubt their capabilities are easily discouraged. Those who have confidence increase their efforts when their performance falls short. They persevere until they succeed. This point is clearly illustrated in a study in which people rated how satisfied or disappointed they were when their performance fell short of their goal, and also rated their level of confidence that they could attain the goal in a second try. They then performed the task again. People who felt disappointed with a deficient performance but were highly confident that they could attain the goal increased their effort to succeed. Those who doubted their capabilities to attain the goal and were too disappointed by their deficient performance abandoned the goal and lost their motivation.[27] This finding gives all the more reason to build competence and confidence, and to create a climate in which people can assume responsibility.

Ensure That Everyone Becomes Responsible

When everyone is a leader, then everyone is responsible for guiding the organization toward its future. Everyone is responsible for maintaining alignment with values. It is not just the job of the person in authority. The whole point of liberating people is so they can take the initiative to do something on their own. When you have liberated the leaders within your constituents, you will see individuals go right to fixing the problem instead of just fixing the blame.

What follow from liberation and the freedom to take initiative are responsibility and accountability for your actions. If everyone is a leader, then everyone accepts the responsibilities of leadership. In this sense, everyone is a citizen, someone who directly participates in enriching and renewing the community. It's as simple as picking up a piece of paper on the streets of your local town, or the hallway, lobby, or plant floor where you work. You could step over it, saying to yourself, "I pay taxes. Public Works should clean it up," or "It's not my job to pick up paper. The maintenance crew picks up the trash." But leaders don't wait for others to do something. They take responsibility for making it happen, even if it means picking up the trash themselves and enlisting others in doing the same.

If you don't think this is critical, consider the situation described by Arun Anand, who was working in Bahrain with a multinational consulting company that had just won a very prestigious vendor due diligence assignment. The scope of work included certain procedures that the local office was not fully accredited to execute, so it sought help from the head office (in London), and the team was assigned to work with a director from the U.K. office. When the project commenced, the local team was enthusiastic because they felt that there would be many opportunities to learn. Arun told us, "Our local director had informed the team that we expected to receive similar assignments in the future and hence it was crucial that every member of the team learned something on this project." What happened? Arun went on to explain:

> While the deliverable on the project was in good shape and the
> U.K. director was able to handle the complex issues that the local
> team was not comfortable with, he did not pass on the knowledge

to the team. He made no attempts to build a climate of trust between himself and the team. He was not prepared to share information and resources; rather, he clearly allocated work in such a way that the team ended up doing only those tasks that they already knew. The challenging areas were handled directly by the director.

The lack of good relationships was evident in the way the team was handled during meetings—even senior members of the local team were not invited by the director for meetings with the client's management. This clearly gave the impression he wanted to keep the local team out of the picture. His discussions with the local office were limited to our partner and senior director and no one else. He was not keen on educating the team on how complex issues needed to be handled. This was exactly the opposite of what we envisaged at the beginning of the assignment when we sought help. He did not structure the task distribution evenly, which would have ensured joint efforts were directed by all towards successful completion.

The consequences of all this were felt even after the deliverable was handed to the client and the U.K. director returned back to the head office. When the client approached us with some queries at a later stage, the local team was not fully equipped to solve them, as they were not aware of the reasons behind certain recommendations provided. This showed our firm in poor light in front of the client, as this reflected the lack of knowledge sharing within the team.

In this instance, the U.K. director did the exact opposite of what a credible leader should do. He not only didn't trust the competence of the local team, he made little effort to enhance its capabilities, which in turn lowered members' morale and confidence. According to Arun, this resulted in "a breach of trust between the local office and the head office, something which will not be forgotten very easily."

By failing to develop capacity, foster collaboration, and facilitate healthy relationships in the team, the U.K. director left the team with no sense of individual accountability and responsibility. Accountability gets to the very core of credibility. It makes it real. Willingness to accept responsibility for one's own actions is the truest test of whether you truly believe what you say.

Capacity building is necessary because people have to be able to "Do What We Say We Will Do." If they can't, then everyone's credibility suffers. That's as true for the CEO or the managing director as it is for the frontline worker, and as true for every single individual as it is for the team. Developing capacity is about building the skills, knowledge, and attitudes of the entire workforce at all levels to DWWSWWD.

The fact that individuals or organizations have the capacity to be consistent with their values does not, however, mean they are. Shared values and shared capacity do not guarantee results. In the final analysis, credibility is earned through credible actions that are supported and consistently reinforced. If a group is to live up to its values, its members must use their skills on a daily basis. For example, your organization may espouse diversity, but if respect for others who are different is not shown on a daily basis—if people of diverse backgrounds are not recruited and hired, if merit reviews don't address accomplishments in the area of diversity, and if performance and rewards are not linked—then diversity becomes just a convenient politically correct slogan.

Credible leaders play a central role in translating promises and preparations into performance. They develop capacity in their organizations, and then they go first, they tell the stories, and they recognize consistent actions. The next chapter takes a look at the leader's role in serving the purpose of the organization and the individuals in it.

DEVELOP CAPACITY
Key Ideas From Chapter Six

- People can't do what they say they will do if they don't know how.

- Credible leaders provide the resources and other organizational supports that enable constituents to build their skills and put their abilities to constructive use.

- Credible leaders foster an ownership mindset by making sure people have choices and the freedom to use their training, their judgment, and their experience to do what is right.

- Credible leaders take actions and create conditions that strengthen everyone's self-esteem and internal sense of effectiveness.

- People can't be expected to learn if they aren't given opportunities to make mistakes.

- Credible leaders share information.

- To build and sustain organizational credibility, credible leaders ensure that everyone accepts responsibility for his or her own actions.

CHAPTER SEVEN

Serve a Purpose

Joanne Chan was working as a pharmacist in Mannings, one of the largest health and beauty retailers in Hong Kong, and her department had consistently failed to meet its profitability targets. Consequently, the regional executive team would not approve expenditures for the computer systems that the local pharmacy team thought necessary for processing prescriptions more efficiently (and profitably). She told us how frustrated and discouraged she and her colleagues felt. And then she told us how Andy, the senior pharmacist, showed them an entirely different perspective:

> He was passionate about his job, and he uplifted and motivated us by telling us that the pharmacy services we provided made a real difference to the company. Andy reassured us that the objective of the pharmacy department was to help patients by providing pharmaceutical services, and that the immediate goal was not to make profits.

To underscore his point, Andy told the team a story about one of the pharmacy's customers, an old lady who had difficulty walking. Whenever she went to the store to seek advice for her health issues, Andy offered her a chair to sit in near the store entrance, so that she did not have to walk all the way to the back of the store where the pharmacy department was located. From her experience with Andy's exceptional customer service, the lady became one of Manning's most loyal customers. "With this example," Joanne said, "Andy shared with us the vision that the pharmacy team was capable of becoming the best group of health care professionals providing excellent services to the general public. By establishing long-term relationships with the patients, we would ultimately generate profits in the future and be able to negotiate with the executives in acquiring the resources we needed."

Andy's passion and storytelling brought that vision to life. What's more, Andy kept reminding his teammates how the pharmacy team was already making a difference to the company and the public. "This made us feel proud of what we did and proud that we belonged to an important organization," Joanne said. "The result of his leadership led to improved performance and profitability of the pharmacy department over the years, and the executive management team eventually approved the installation of the computer systems, which greatly improved the performance of the pharmacy team."

Joanne's experience with Andy illustrates what happens when leaders adopt the view that their role is to serve and not to be served. Alan Mulally, president and CEO of the Ford Motor Company, made that point directly. When asked by the *Washington Post*, "How has your leadership style changed over the years? What have you learned? What do you know now that you didn't use to?" Alan responded,

> I think that just always remembering that we're here to serve. We have the honor to be selected to be the leader, but we're actually serving our customers, we're serving our employees, and the more that you have a servant perspective or a servant attitude, then the more inclusion you'll have, the more respect for people's ideas [you'll have]. You'll seek to understand before you seek to be understood.[1]

Alan maintained that this servant attitude played a large part in the turnaround process at Ford during the difficult years at the end of the twenty-first century's opening decade.

Credible leaders serve a purpose, and they serve the people who have made it possible for them to lead. They put the guiding principles of the organization ahead of all else, and then strive to live by those principles. They set the example for others and are the first to do what has been agreed upon. In serving a purpose, you strengthen credibility by demonstrating that you are not in it for yourself but instead have the interests of the institution, department, or team and its constituents at heart. Being a servant may not be what you had in mind when you chose to take responsibility for the vision and direction of your team, but serving others is the most glorious and rewarding of all leadership tasks.

The concept of "servant leadership" is not new. Many years ago Robert Greenleaf pointed out, "The great leader is seen as servant first, and that simple fact is the key to [the leader's] greatness."[2] Robert, who had spent thirty years as a Fortune 50 senior executive, spent the last part of his career reflecting upon and organizing what he had learned about successful business and professional people. He observed that those people who believed foremost in the concept of service, who were servant leaders, were also successful leaders. It was their belief in serving others that enabled these executives to provide leadership that made others willing to follow.

Seeing a new kind of connection between leaders and their constituents, Robert suggested:

> A new moral principle is emerging which holds that the only authority deserving one's allegiance is that which is freely and knowingly granted by the led to the leader in response to, and in proportion to, the clearly evident servant stature of the leader. Those who choose to follow this principle will not casually accept

the authority of existing institutions. Rather, they will freely respond only to individuals who are chosen as leaders because they are proven and trusted as servants.[3]

Three and a half decades later, Charlene Li, founder of the Altimeter Group and one of the world's foremost experts on social media, commented that Robert Greenleaf "turned leadership on its head, positioning executives as humble stewards of the corporation, not the almighty heads of them." Then she offered this: "What's changed today is that the new technologies allow us to let go of control and still be in command. . . . The result of these new relationships is *open leadership*, which I define as: *having the confidence and humility to give up the need to be in control while inspiring commitment from people to accomplish goals*."[4] (Italics hers.) In the last quarter-century the world has seen the creation of tools that make servant leadership more than a theory; they make it a necessity. Only when leaders turn leadership on its head and truly understand that they do not have the same top-down authority that they once did—and that a more open approach to leadership is the new normal—will they fully realize the potential of a more open society and the powerful social media technologies that enable it.

Servant leaders put other people's needs first. Their measure of success is whether those who are served grow—whether they become healthier, wiser, freer, more autonomous, more capable—and whether they are more likely themselves to become servant leaders in their own right. This is not the image you see on reality TV, but it is the way things work in the real world. People will not voluntarily follow self-serving leaders whose goals are to enrich only themselves. People want to follow leaders who place others' interests above their own.

The truth is that you either lead by example or you don't lead at all.[5] Credible leaders walk the talk. They don't ask others to do something they wouldn't do themselves. Credible leaders hold themselves accountable to the same set of standards as they hold others.

When Chuck Berger, CEO of several troubled start-ups over his career, was asked how he gets others on his team to work so hard and care deeply about what they are doing, he was quick to respond that leading by example is "exactly what I do. If folks were to see me going out the door at 2:00 PM you can be sure they wouldn't be fired up to stick around and work all that hard themselves."[6] You have to go first—and *not* out the door, unless that's where you want others to go.

Go First

Leaders take the first step because doing so provides tangible evidence of their commitment. By going first, leaders serve their constituents' desire to know what's acceptable and what's not. Leaders are visible models of what to do and what not to do. And that means they should be models of what they want. One of the most important ways human beings learn is by observing others, and leaders had better be superb examples of the kind of behavior that's expected. Whether your constituents say it out loud or not, they are often saying to themselves things like, "You said we should be innovative. Exactly what does innovative look like around here?" Or "You said we should be collaborative and work together as a team. How do we do that?" Your behavior should answer their questions.

As expressed in the Chinese proverb "the lower beam will not be level if the upper one is not," what leaders *do* is the single most important factor in demonstrating to others what is, and is not, acceptable behavior in their teams and organizations. That's why it's so important to set a positive example of what you expect from others. Your behavior is how people calibrate their own behaviors and choices. It's also what generates intensity around shared values. For shared values to make a difference in how the organization runs, the leader must adhere to them—and must do so in ways that are clearly evident to constituents. Researchers have found that organizations where employees strongly believe their managers follow through on promises and demonstrate the values they preach are substantially more profitable than those organizations whose managers scored average or lower on these dimensions.[7]

Stephen Tam learned firsthand the importance of leaders going first while he was interning with the Southern California district office of Bridgestone Americas, Inc. Each district director oversaw twelve retail stores, principally acting as the management level between the stores and regional management. While every district office had its own set of flexible rules and guidelines on how to operate, they remained responsible for meeting the company's overall goal of continuously improving car service quality and customer satisfaction levels, since these had been identified as driving business growth. Stephen observed the powerful impact of the district director's decision to put words into action by implementing a new policy: once every two weeks the director and the deputy lieutenants at the district office would get their hands dirty working at separate retail locations, changing tires and performing other car service tasks as well as working the front desk to interact with customers. As Stephen explained:

> The district director demonstrated to his employees that he and his deputy lieutenants understood the value of customer service and quality car service, and demonstrated it by sacrificing a busy day on a biweekly basis to work on the front line to handle customers like store associates. He wanted the store managers and associates to know that the district office understood the importance of our key strategies for success and did not just bark orders from their district "glass tower." The director followed through on initiatives he preached by actually doing them for all his employees to see.

How you spend your time, as Stephen witnessed, is one of the clearest signals you can send about what you think is important and is the truest, most tangible indicator of your priorities. That Bridgestone district director made sure to spend his own time doing exactly what he was telling everyone else was important: serving the customer. Little wonder that within a short time of his assuming leadership for that district it became one of the top five in its region.

Constituents measure how serious their leaders are about key values by observing how much time they spend on them. Management guru Tom Peters, who coauthored the best-selling book *In Search of Excellence* and has written many other influential management titles, has said, "Your calendar never lies.... *Time is your only true resource....* And the way you divvy time up—visible to one and all—is the only true statement of what really matters to you."[8] It's not likely that anyone will take their manager's exhortations about, say, innovation, seriously when no one can remember seeing that individual do anything new or different or devote any time in meetings to talking about new products or services.

How shared values are actually put into practice becomes crystal clear during critical incidents.[9] These incidents require leaders to step in and make decisions based on matters of principle. Often the most dramatic are when a key value is at stake or when someone's behavior is inconsistent with the stated values. In taking a difficult stand or confronting a challenging situation leaders let others know that they are willing to put their personal career or personal safety on the line in service of shared values.

Arun Anand's experience on his company's U.S. GAAP (Generally Accepted Accounting Principles) team underscored the fact that the way leaders perform under pressure is the way their constituents will also perform. It was, in Arun's words, "crisis time"—they had less than two days left before their earnings release was due. The whole team was in low spirits and demotivated, with a ton of work still to be done. "This was an occasion when everyone," Arun said, "was looking to our vice president to demonstrate his leadership skills!" What happened?

As a first step, the VP brought the entire team together in one room and told them that this was the time that they were going to prove that they could stand up to a challenge. He reasoned that this was the moment for them to stand together and stay committed to the objective of completing their part on time. "Normally," Arun says, "a VP is not required to personally be involved in the preparation of the financial statements, but in this case he took upon himself the responsibility to ensure that the task was accomplished." And what did his personal involvement illustrate to the team? According to Arun:

> [It demonstrated] his "inner values" and especially how he was committed to the results of the team. It was this inner value of showing commitment that guided his action. The VP also gave a pep talk to the team to reinforce that they could do what was required of them. This style of instilling the core values into his team affirmed our shared values and forged unity amongst us. After motivating the team, the VP went about the task in a thoroughly professional manner. He worked together with every team member to ensure that there were no bottlenecks. In the end, the financial statements were completed on time and there were no further setbacks.

Arun's experience substantiates that the way leaders behave, especially in difficult times, has a huge impact on the performance of others. When these moments occur they represent great teaching opportunities. They are moments, sometimes large and sometimes small, when you, both as a leader and as a constituent, put your credibility on the line. They force you to ask yourself: Do I do what I say I will do?

Stay in Touch

As we've said repeatedly, leadership is a relationship. To remain strong the relationship has to be nurtured. You can't do that from a distance, and you can't do that every once in a while. You have to stay in touch, and you have to stay in touch often. You have to do it with family and friends, and you have to do it with constituents. Leader credibility is earned through human contact—in hallways, on factory floors, in retail shops, in classrooms, and on the streets. It's earned when you shake a hand, ask a question, and listen to what others have to say. While social media tools are useful means of staying in touch with those who are remote, when it comes to strengthening your credibility there is just no substitute for those eye-to-eye and ear-to-ear connections.

Staying in touch starts with listening. With so much emphasis on how important it is for leaders to make effective presentations, you might get the impression that the best leaders are the best talkers. In fact, talking is highly overrated. Listening is far more important to effective leadership. Impressive listening skill is one of the core competencies of credible leaders. Leadership authors Liz Wiseman and Greg McKeown, for example, report that the leaders they call "multipliers"—leaders who make others around them smarter and more capable—"are ferocious listeners [who] . . . don't just listen the majority of the time. They massively shift the ratio, listening most of the time."[10]

It's easy to understand why leaders who listen are more credible than those who talk, talk, and talk. The more the leader talks, the less other people can contribute. The less others can contribute, the less they want to contribute the next time they're with the leader who doesn't listen. Listening also keeps leaders from becoming isolated and removed from critical information. But how does it help leaders earn credibility? Simple. Listening demonstrates to others that you are interested in

140

them. Listening demonstrates that you are receptive to other people's ideas and opinions. Listening demonstrates you trust others. Listening demonstrates you care. When other people believe you trust them and care about them they are more likely to trust you.

Sometimes when you listen you get good news. Then there are times when you get bad news. When things are going well, it's not all that difficult to hear the news. But it's how you react to news about mistakes, difficulties, and problems that may be the better indicator of whether or not constituents feel they can trust you. From the constituent's perspective, the question is always: "If I'm the messenger with bad news, what will happen to me if I bring it forward?"

Even if the news makes your blood boil, you need to remain calm, ask even-tempered questions, and be able, with sincerity, to thank the person for bringing this unpleasant (but never unwanted) information to your attention. When serving a purpose (rather than a personal agenda), you can adopt the posture that the "facts are friendly" and appreciate that without valid and reliable information, your ability to be an effective problem solver is diminished. You must enable people to feel that they can discuss anything with you, without having to mince words or fear upsetting you. The focus should be not on whether or how someone screwed up (even, or especially, you), but on making sure that the right thing is done.

Staying in touch requires more than just listening; it also means that leaders must remain approachable. This involves never giving the appearance that you're so busy that you have no time to talk with anyone who isn't already on the schedule—or that your schedule is so full that people have to wait so long to get an appointment that they lose interest in the issue, and in you. Consider seriously doing away with any imperial trappings associated with your position (the cavernous office, the executive dining room, the dark-windowed limo) because these also make you appear distant and inaccessible. Establish regular times on your calendar when people know they can come to see you. Be careful that you don't book your daily or weekly calendar so full that people who want—or need—to talk with you can't get on your schedule. Even better, go to their offices or pick up your phone and give them a call. Take one or more of your constituents out for the occasional lunch or dinner with no set agenda other than just a little friendly "What's on your mind?"

Every month President Michael Engh, S.J., for example, invites six to ten of his Santa Clara University faculty and staff colleagues to join him for coffee and some informal conversation about what's going on around campus. Leaders who want to stay in touch with their constituents always have time to get out of their offices to step down the hall, walk over to the lab, or visit the plant to find out what is going on.

Make Meaning, Daily

Credible leaders are always present in the minds and hearts of their constituents. Jim Shunk, vice president of Human Resources for Maxygen/Perseid, illustrated how profound this presence can be. In handling his own difficult situations, he told us, he still finds himself recalling how one of his most admired leaders behaved:

> I remember how he could let people vent their feelings and anger—yell and scream as if he had personally caused their problem—and still listen calmly and with empathy. And when we'd done something that was right (proper or legal) but it still wasn't the right (fair) thing, he'd move mountains to rectify the situation for one and all. Whenever I'm in doubt, I still think about what he would say and do.

Leaders make impressions. They leave footprints—and these prints become guides for those who come behind them, whether a new project engineer or veteran personnel director. To the extent that people have positive and consistent images of their leaders in their heads, they will want to be like them, and act in ways that are consistent with shared values. In contrast, if their leaders are inconsistent and inconsiderate, people will not want to emulate them or put into practice the values their leaders only give lip service to.

One of the purposes leaders serve is to help people make choices and to make sense of things. Sometimes that comes in a one-on-one conversation when a direct report asks, "What should I do in this situation?" But more often than not, it comes from recalling the lessons we've learned from a leader in days past. It's like Jim said, "Whenever I'm in doubt, I still think about what he would say and do." When people are confronted with confusing situations, they seek guidance from those they admire and respect. They look to them for answers. That guidance can't always be in person. But that person can be present in their minds. This is why it is so vitally important for leaders to be exemplary role models for the values and principles that they represent. Leaders teach by example. They provide illustrations of appropriate behavior that constituents mentally store away for retrieval later on. Then, when people are looking for guidance, and they think about what one of their admired leaders did in a similar situation, they'll find relevant examples of how to respond. They'll find ways to make sense of new and challenging situations.

In the course of your everyday comings and goings you have many opportunities to be visibly credible by standing up on behalf of shared values and demonstrating your commitment to a shared purpose. Many of these occasions are small incidents, such as the way you greet someone on the telephone, handle an interruption, bring up an idea, or introduce one associate to another. Probably no single one of these behaviors makes a difference by itself, but over the course of time your daily, and often mundane, actions add up and present an easily recognized pattern or way of being that either promotes or discourages trust. People learn whether or not they can count on their leaders by watching them operate across a wide variety of settings. Consistency reveals both a depth of conviction and an internal integration between words and actions. Promises are made easily enough, but are they kept?

Think about the leadership lesson that one young project engineer learned from his first manager, someone he felt—despite having several hundred people reporting to him—"didn't really have much of a clue about what it meant to be a leader." This engineer backed up this assessment with an illustration about how disconnected his manager's words and actions were with the organization's values:

> Ours is a heavy equipment industry, and therefore safety plays a huge role in everyday working life. There is always danger lurking about, and everyone must be conscious of their surrounding environment. As a result, every year, the company's executive team visits the field installations for a walk-about. The walk-about involves having all employees break up into teams of ten, with each team having one executive member from head office. The purpose of the walk-about is to identify "points of danger" where someone could get hurt. For example, a manhole left open and unmarked or an employee without a safety vest. This was a way for the head office to get involved hands-on with the safety effort. Of course, safety was something that was pushed by the head office year round, but once a year the executives wanted to really drive the message home and they did this by participating in the walk-about.
>
> My boss would always complain about the walk-about and say things like "I don't have time to waste an entire day walking around looking for open manholes" or simply exclaim, "This is such a waste of time." He would begrudgingly assign us into teams for the walk-about and then go into the field to remind the unionized employees that the "executives were on the way, so safety was now important today."

These were terrible messages because it clearly showed that he had no respect for the company's message of safety and he was setting an example to those of us that worked for him that the walk-about was a joke and not pertinent to our work lives.

As a result, the engineer explained, their office never felt fully aligned with the company's standards: "We always felt like we were on a separate ship with our own agenda and priorities." As a new member of the team, he said:

> I felt extremely confused about the safety message. I knew that safety was important, but my boss was making a joke of it, passing on conflicting messages. The result was that the entire office made light of the situation and you could hear jokes daily about the "waste of time walk-about." Basically, the employees followed suit; if the manager wasn't taking this seriously, why should we?

This engineer is not alone; people make meaning of their situations by paying attention to the actions of their leaders, and especially to the congruence or disconnect between their words and their behaviors. The takeaway lesson from this project engineer's experience with his manager is a good reminder that people are watching and paying attention to everything you do:

> What I learned from this is that if I am a leader, I need to be very careful about what I say and what I do, because my team will watch me carefully and more likely than not mirror the example that I set.

It is important to think carefully about the meaning you are creating with your actions. Making meaning is one of the most critical tasks for leaders in serving a purpose. Whatever the purpose, leaders attempt to create a meaning with sufficient emotional impact that their constituents will be confident and excited about the endeavor.

145

Become a Storyteller

The ancient art of storytelling is another major way that leaders teach others about what sense to make of various actions and achievements. Many of the stories come from their own experiences of going first, taking risks, and confronting critical incidents. Many come from what team members have done, and still others from leaders they've observed in other settings. Stories are teaching tools and powerful strategies for getting your point across, and your constituents will remember them better than policy pronouncements, lists, or statistics.[11] The latter are typically abstract and bland, lacking the emotional stickiness that makes them memorable. Stories, on the other hand, are examples of what the policies or principles look like in action. They are the narrative that's needed to bring things to life.

Stories, analogies, and metaphors have a substantial impact on decision making; information is more quickly and accurately remembered when it is first presented in the form of an example or story, particularly one that is intrinsically appealing.[12] Scholars point out that a leader's words "often assume their greatest impact as symbols rather than as literal meanings."[13] This is especially true when those words are used to tell a story. Stories serve as kind of a mental map that helps people know, first, what is important (that is, purpose and values) and, second, how things are done in a particular group or organization.

In his book *Managing by Storying Around*, the late David Armstrong, CEO and president of Armstrong International, offered numerous reasons why storytelling is an effective leadership practice. It's simple: anyone can tell a story. It's timeless: stories are fad proof. It's appealing to everyone: everybody, regardless of age, gender, or race, listens to stories. It's fun: stories are friendly and enjoyable. In addition, storytelling is a useful form of training, a good method for empowering people, an effective recognition device, a good recruiting and hiring tool, a useful sales technique, and an excellent way to pass along corporate traditions.[14] An added benefit is that telling stories forces you to pay keen attention to what your constituents are doing. To find a good story, you need to be on the lookout for someone who is doing something to contribute to your group's expectations.

There are several things you can do to be a good storyteller. For example, tell personal stories. A story that involves you or that your audience can personally relate to has more impact than an abstract third-person example. Talk from a first-person perspective. If you are feeling truly excited about a particular activity or goal, show it. If you are deeply concerned about competitive threats, show it. Allowing your emotions to surface brings excitement to your voice and increases your natural tendency to use gestures and to smile (generally lighting up your face). Start your story by relating a heroic deed. Think of a clever title for the story to capture people's attention; this helps them to remember (catalogue) it. Give your story a theme and be willing to repeat this theme. Keep the story short. Use people's names. Verify all the facts. Be sure to end your message or story with its moral: a conclusion that concretely demonstrates the message or lesson you intend to be learned from this story.[15] Becoming a good storyteller enables the purpose you are striving to serve to live on long after you personally are no longer on the scene.

Regain Credibility Lost

Despite everyone's best intentions, despite the pursuit of flawless leadership, and despite efforts to be open and humble, things don't always go as planned, expected, or promised. Sometimes circumstances change, and you can no longer do what you said you would do.

Sometimes you realize, probably belatedly, that you don't have the competence or resources to do what you said. Sometimes you and others make errors in judgment or choose the wrong strategies. Sometimes you just mess up. No human being is exempt from failure. The trouble is that leadership failures and human frailties can sometimes seriously damage your credibility. So it's important to understand what you can do to regain credibility if ever you should tarnish or lose it.

Pradeep Vaswani, project manager at Infosys Technologies, recalled a time when his team went off course and as a result would fail to deliver on time to the client. His managers had advised him that he shouldn't disclose this in advance to their client, but should merely work overtime to catch up. However, Pradeep knew that keeping this secret would result in a breach of trust with his client if the matter went out of control. Furthermore, he was unwilling to set such a poor example to his staff. Consequently, Pradeep accepted the responsibility for informing the client about the project's status.

The client was upset, but Pradeep also told them how sorry and disappointed he and his team were about missing the deadline. He explained what had caused the delay and what the team would do. He showed his commitment to the new deadline by indicating what he would do himself to ensure the new deliverables were met. The project was completed by the new deadline, and the amount of trust the client had for Pradeep actually increased tremendously. At the same time the respect his team members had for him was enhanced because he accepted responsibility and showed accountability for the team without pointing fingers.[16]

In searching for guidelines on how to recover from failures of leadership, you can learn a great deal by observing how confidence is regained after a service failure. The good news is that, as customer service researchers have documented, "satisfactory problem resolution sharply increases customers' willingness to recommend the company and significantly improves their perception of the company's service quality."[17] When leaders satisfactorily respond to their failures of leadership, constituents are willing to continue to follow and trust them. Recovering from mistakes that damage leadership credibility is similar to service recovery, except that the stakes are often much higher. To increase your chances for regaining the trust of your constituents after acting in a way that diminishes your credibility, you need to follow the "Six A's of Leadership Accountability": accept, admit, apologize, act, amend, and attend.[18]

When people are asked what's the most important thing a leader should do after making a mistake, the universal response is "admit it." To admit means that you first have to accept personal responsibility for your actions, and, in the case of leaders, the actions of your organization. Then you have to publicly acknowledge that you have made a mistake. But because of concerns of legal exposure or a mistaken fear that admitting a mistake may hurt credibility, many times leaders either deny or attempt to cover up any wrongdoing, thus ensuring even more damage to their reputations.

But doesn't admitting mistakes damage credibility? If clients and colleagues know you have failed, won't they be more likely to think you are incompetent? Evidence shows that attempting to hide mistakes is much more damaging and is much more likely to erode credibility. In our research "admits mistakes" was mentioned second only to "tells the truth" when people were asked to explain what behaviors best define an honest person. There's no better way to demonstrate your honesty to your constituents than owning up to your mistakes. By admitting you're wrong—and then doing something about it—you can strengthen your credibility rather than diminish it.

Offering an apology is another important step in rebuilding credibility. It lets constituents know that you are concerned about the impact your actions may have had on them, as well as the problems your actions may have caused them. Quick action to deal with the immediate consequences of a mistake needs to follow an apology. A quick response lets others know that you are going to do something about the problem, and do it now. If possible, get others involved at this stage. Sharing the problem and asking for suggestions tells others that you trust their judgment in tough times; this appreciation for the talents of others contributes to leadership credibility.

Making amends for mistakes is a necessary but often overlooked part of the rebuilding process. In service recovery this is often referred to as "atonement." A leader's error can cause hardship to others. A poor choice of strategy or failure to respond to competitive threats may cost jobs or require cuts in expenses. If other people are going to suffer in some way, the leader should suffer also. People don't expect you to resign for an honest error or lapse in judgment, but they do expect some form of reparation or personal participation in the hardship. The amends should fit the problem.

And finally, to make sure that you are attuned to the influence your actions are having on restoring lost credibility, you should pay close attention to the reactions of your constituents. Ask for their feedback and be as nondefensive as you can be in listening to constructive criticism. Attending helps to determine if the recovery actions are working and if anything else may need to be done to rebuild your credibility in their eyes.

Constituents tend to be forgiving—up to a point. To use a typically American aphorism, the "three strikes and you're out" rule seems to govern how many mistakes leaders can make before losing their credibility. The first time a leader makes a mistake, people can fault the process or perhaps that the person was new to the job. "He's still learning," they might say. "Everyone makes mistakes." The second time, people might say the leader didn't have the necessary skills or was a slow learner. But after the third miss, people tend to conclude that the leader is beyond help and is not deserving of continued allegiance. The problem begins to be seen as part of a recurring pattern of personal shortcomings.

Excellent recovery is no substitute for weak leadership. Your reputation for being a strong and credible leader depends upon continuous attention to the disciplines of discovering, appreciating, affirming, developing, serving, and sustaining. But when those inevitable mistakes or lapses do occur, a thorough recovery effort can renew your leadership reputation.

In serving a purpose, leaders earn their credibility by going first, whether it's admitting a mistake or teaching others what to do. Servant leadership is about spending time and investing energy in setting a positive example. It is about sharing stories of exemplary performance, standing up for your beliefs, and confronting critical incidents. This is how leaders give meaning to shared values.

Leaders also have to deal directly with the cynicism, frustration, and despair that constituents may feel, and that is the focus of the next chapter: how to keep hope alive.

SERVE A PURPOSE
Key Ideas From Chapter Seven

- Credible leaders put the guiding principles of the organization ahead of everything else.

- Credible leaders are the first to do what has been agreed upon.

- In taking the first step, credible leaders provide tangible evidence of their commitment and are visible models of the kinds of behaviors that are expected.

- To sustain credibility, credible leaders stay in touch.

- People make meaning of their situations by paying attention to the actions of their leaders, and especially to the congruence or disconnect between their words and their behaviors.

- Storytelling is a major way that leaders teach others about what sense or meaning to make of various actions and achievements.

- Even the best leaders mess up.

- Credible leaders know what to do to regain credibility if they undermine or lose it.

CHAPTER EIGHT

Sustain Hope

W hen leaders uplift spirits and restore people's belief in the future, they strengthen their own credibility.[1] Constituents want leaders who demonstrate an enthusiastic and genuine belief in the capacity of others, who strengthen people's will, who supply the means to achieve, and who express optimism for the future. Constituents want leaders who remain passionate despite obstacles and setbacks. In uncertain times, leaders with a positive, confident, can-do approach are desperately needed in business and in life.

Salvatore Sarno is a compelling example of how a leader can uplift people's spirits.[2] Salvatore is the managing director of the team driving *Shosholoza*, the first African boat to take part in the most important sailing competition in the world, the America's Cup race. Salvatore's biggest passion is sailing, and for many years before the official launch of the *Shosholoza* initiative he would talk about his dream: "One day we will participate in the America's Cup. I want to give to these guys the opportunity to make history."

For many people Salvatore's idea was crazy and disruptive, but not only did he believe in it deeply, he also communicated and shared his vision passionately with the people around him. His dream went far beyond the sport experience: he not only wanted South Africa to be the first African team in the America's Cup, he wanted to give a chance to people who had grown up under difficult conditions to represent the pride of their nation in front of the world. What's more, he wanted to demonstrate to South Africans—and to the world—that with hope and the passion that accompanies it, you can overcome the most difficult of problems.

In 2007 *Shosholoza* took part in the America's Cup race, a remarkable achievement in itself since only twelve countries were represented. *Shosholoza*, with a significantly lower budget and less experience than the world giants like *Alinghi, Oracle*, or *Luna Rossa*, managed to compete at the same level as the other eleven participants. Placing sixth at the final round in Valencia, the South African team had achieved some amazing victories in heads-up challenges against giants like *Luna Rossa* and *Mascalzone Latino*.

These achievements reached far beyond the results on the race-course, however. *Shosholoza* became a "hope generator" for many South Africans who identified in this success with pride. And the spread of optimism didn't stop at the America's Cup success. Thanks to the creation of MSC-Shosholoza Foundation sailing centers around South Africa, less wealthy youths of all races are able to learn sailing and life skills.[3] The meaning of the team's name is an acknowledgment of the dedication to pursue excellence, especially when the struggle is a challenge—the Zulu word *shosholoza* means "go forward, make your road, forge ahead." The spirit of the *Shosholoza* projects is all about keeping hope alive and taking concrete action to achieve the dream.

Leaders must keep hope alive. They must strengthen people's belief that the struggle they are called upon to deal with will produce a more promising future. The only antidote to the increased cynicism and stresses of these times is renewed faith in human capacity and an intensely optimistic belief that together leaders and constituents can overcome the difficulties of today and tomorrow. "Keep hope alive" continues to be the credible leader's battle cry.

Hope is essential to achieving the highest levels of performance. Studies clearly show that people with high hope have a greater number of goals across various arenas of life, select more difficult goals, and see their goals in a more challenging and positive manner than people with low hope.[4]

Keeping hope alive is also essential to an active and healthy life. In some of the most dramatic studies of hope, researchers examined depression and psychosocial impairment among men and women with traumatically acquired spinal cord injuries. They found that patients who exhibited more hope had less depression, greater mobility (despite similar injuries), and more social contacts. In short, they reported that "those with high hope were more adaptive in all realms, regardless of how long they had been injured, whether just a month or 40 years."[5]

Similar links have been made between optimism (a sibling of hope) and health. In a longitudinal study of healthy and successful members of the Harvard classes of 1942 through 1944, researchers examined the link between optimism and health. They concluded that "optimism early in life is associated with good health later in life."[6] Other research reveals that pessimistic college students visited the doctor nearly three times as often as their optimistic peers, and the pessimists were ill more than twice the number of days. Optimists also live longer following heart attacks and after the diagnosis of cancer.[7] Optimism pays off in a more healthy life.

Credible leaders sustain hope by painting positive images of the future. They arouse optimistic feelings and enable their constituents to hold positive thoughts about the possibilities of success. These leaders also struggle alongside others. They neither are immune to nor hide from the suffering. In keeping hope alive, credible leaders demonstrate their faith and confidence by first accepting responsibility for the quality of their lives and for the lives of their constituents. Even when everything goes wrong or when resounding defeats occur, credible leaders bounce back by taking charge of the situation. And credible leaders keep hope alive when they recognize the dedication of others to pursue excellence, especially when the struggle is difficult and challenging.

Take Charge

A fierce determination to succeed is characteristic of survivors and thrivers in all arenas. The late Sam Walton (founder of Walmart, the world's largest retailer) and *Shosholoza*'s Salvatore Sarno may be oceans apart on politics and industries, but they're members of the same crew when it comes to optimism, determination, drive, and resilience. When Sam opened his very first retail operation—a little Ben Franklin franchise store in Newport, Arkansas—he wanted to build it into the best store in town, and he did. It was so successful, in fact, that his landlord wanted it for himself and his son. The landlord put the squeeze on Sam and did not renew the lease, knowing Sam had no other place to go in the small town. Instead, he offered to buy the franchise. Sam had no choice in that instance but to give up the store and move on. Sam said, "It was the low point in my business life. . . . It really was like a nightmare. I had built the best variety store in the whole region and worked hard in the community—done everything right—and now I was being kicked out of town."

But Sam was not down for long. "It's not just a corny saying that you can make a positive out of most any negative if you work at it hard enough. I've always thought of problems as challenges, and this one wasn't any different. . . . I had to pick myself up and get on with it, do it all over again, only even better this time."[8]

It is this attitude—making positives out of negatives, thinking of problems as challenges, working hard, and doing even better—as much as retailing savvy (in Sam's case) or sailing prowess (in Salvatore's) that enables leaders to succeed. They see setbacks and defeats as temporary challenges that can be overcome by personal passion, will, and courage. They demonstrate that by defying the verdict, constantly exhibiting courage, and actively tackling the work required—all while maintaining a sense of humor—they can triumph over adversity. And such leaders inspire others to do the same.

Credible leaders are proactive. They do not wait to be told what to do. They believe that it is possible to exert internal control, rather than being controlled externally by others or events. They recognize that while they cannot control 100 percent of what goes on in life, they are determined to be in charge of the quality of their own lives. Maybe the company has no overarching vision or plan; for credible leaders, even this is not an insurmountable roadblock. They search for their own opportunities to make something happen—and they instill this attitude in constituents, creating ways people can take charge of at least their own twenty-five square feet.

In *Head First: The Biology of Hope*, the late Norman Cousins observed that when presented with a serious diagnosis, some cancer patients "responded with a fierce determination to overcome."

> They didn't deny the diagnosis. They denied the verdict that is usually associated with it. Was it any coincidence that a substantial number of these patients lived significantly longer than had been predicted by their oncologists?[9]

Similarly, credible leaders, just like Sam and Salvatore, behave like survivors. They acknowledge reality but do not dwell on the threat. Instead they see change as a challenge and an opportunity for renaissance and learning; they move quickly to mobilize personal and group resources. They believe they can influence the outcome and can turn the tide of events to their advantage. They do not become resentful, bitter, or alienated; instead, they become engaged, involved, and committed. They do not dissolve into despair—they resolve to act quickly and zestfully.[10]

It would be foolish for people to ignore the fact that they have life-threatening diseases, or that their businesses are failing, or that their marriages are troubled. It would be foolish to deny the changes in their bodies, or organizations, or families. Leaders must listen to the diagnosis; they must listen to the reality, particularly in cases of adversity.

But acknowledging the reality does not mean you must accept the verdict. You can be well informed and deeply understand the peril you face without accepting a prognosis that your organization or civilization is doomed. Reality may mean that you have lost a loved one or that you are disabled by a physical trauma; it does not have to mean that you have been sentenced to a life of misery. Reality may mean that the world is plagued by poverty, pollution, unemployment, riots, and infectious disease. But it does not have to mean that civilized society is coming to an end. Reality may mean that the restaurant's menu is not working, or that the warehouses were destroyed, or that you just got restructured out of a job. It does not have to mean that companies will go bankrupt or that business careers are over.

Just like survivors of serious injury and illness, credible leaders accept the diagnosis, but they do not accept defeat; they do not become consumed by self-pity and grief. They regroup, reassess, and prepare to go forward. Leaders inspire others by sharing their determination to beat the odds. Take it from Carolina Rojas, who met her most admired leader when she was working with PepsiCo Mexico. She told us that he had a "Yes, it is possible" attitude. "While this outlook won't make problems disappear," she said, "it helps me and others to believe the future will be better. In addition, this positive thinking lets you discover an amazing power from people when they think in this way."

This is not just a matter of "Where there's a will there's a way." This old folk wisdom is only half correct, says psychologist and researcher Charles Snyder. Hope, he has found, "means believing you have both the will and the way to accomplish your goals, whatever they may be."[11] It takes both a will and a way—or waypower and willpower as Charles would say—to achieve what Sam and Salvatore did. It takes both to thrive in a volatile and dynamic business environment.

Researchers refer to this take-charge attitude as *grit*, and they are finding that it plays an essential role in attaining difficult goals. Angela Duckworth, professor of psychology at the University of Pennsylvania, and her colleagues define grit very simply as "perseverance and passion for long-term goals" and report that it "entails working strenuously toward challenges, maintaining effort and interest over years despite failure, adversity, and plateaus in progress."[12] They've developed a test to measure it, asking about such things as setting goals, being obsessed with an idea or project, maintaining focus, sticking with things that take a long time to complete, overcoming setbacks, and the like. They've studied the grit of kids in school, cadets in the military, working professionals, artists, academics, and others. Their results convincingly demonstrate that people who have the most grit are the ones most likely to achieve positive outcomes. As Angela notes, "I'll bet that there isn't a single successful person who hasn't depended on grit. Nobody is talented enough to not have to work hard, and that's what grit allows you to do."[13] To be the most successful, you and your constituents must take charge by having passion for a purpose and the perseverance to hang in there for the long term.

159

Balance Hope and Work

Whatever your hope—freedom, peace, justice, happiness, quality, progress, clean air, technical superiority, business success, or even good grades in school—you have to work for it. And the more hope you have, the more work (and grit) you need.

Best-selling author and social activist Rita Mae Brown has certainly had her beliefs severely tested. Her good grades got her a scholarship to the University of Florida—and her civil-rights activism got her thrown out. Her diligence earned her a doctorate from the Institute for Policy Studies in Washington, D.C.—and her questioning attitude got her in trouble. Both the FBI and the CIA kept files on her. It is no wonder that Rita Mae wrote, "People are like tea bags; you never know how strong they'll be until they're in hot water. In times of trouble, you not only discover what you truly believe but whether or not you can act on your beliefs."[14]

Rita Mae connects grit and hope with action, everyday actions. This insight means, as she explained, "I believe you never hope more than you work. In action, this means I work ten to sixteen hours a day, usually seven days a week. Since I love my work . . . this is a joy. I believe you are your work. Don't trade the very stuff of your life, time, for nothing more than dollars. That's a rotten bargain."[15]

If you hope more than you work, you and your constituents are likely to be very disappointed. And your credibility is likely to suffer. But some ask, "What about balance?" Don't good leaders have balance in their lives? Certainly they do. However, balance is relative: each individual has a personal definition. No one can determine if another's life is out of balance without knowing the weights and measures in that person's life. If a leader, for example, loads up one side of the scale with a ton of hope, the only way to get life to be in balance is to load the other with a ton of work. Anything less would surely bring disappointment. However, if a leader has only an ounce of hope and loads the scale with a ton of work, the scale is out of balance. The secret to balance seems to be to not overload the scale on either end. When hope and work, challenge and skills are in balance, that's when you experience optimal performance.[16]

People with high hope are not Pollyannas. They are not blind to the realities of the present. If something isn't working or if the current methods aren't effective, they don't ignore it, cross their fingers, or simply redouble their efforts. They assess the situation and find new ways to reach the goals. And if the goals begin to recede rather than draw closer, people with hope reset their goals.[17]

Changing the strategy or aiming for another target is not defeatism. In fact, if a leader persists in a strategy that doesn't work or fixates on one goal that is blocked, constituents can become frustrated and depressed, leading them to feel defeated rather than victorious. You can't strengthen your credibility by continuing to do what you said you would do if what you are doing isn't working. It is better to find a new path or decide on a new destination. Then once that end is reached, set a new, more challenging objective. Admitting that you are wrong and finding a better course of action is a far more courageous as well as more credible path to take.

Sometimes the best answer, according to Emily Abrera, an icon in the Philippines advertising industry for her work with McCann-Erickson (chairman emeritus) and serving now in the public sector in charge of the Board of the Cultural Center of the Philippines as well as the Children's Hour Foundation, is to find balance in laughter. "Laughing at yourself," Emily said, "helps to maintain your humanity." Credible leaders have a sense of humor; they are able to laugh at themselves and their troubles. Being able to laugh even in the most stressful of times helps people thrive, and science is proving that laughter releases the body's natural healing powers.[18] Credible leaders find the comic in the tragic. They make it okay to have some fun even when times are tough. They know that laughing—especially when you are low—uplifts the spirits. Humorless people who take things too seriously are likely to dig themselves into deep holes of despair. And they bury everyone around them in the process.

Arouse Positive Thoughts and Images

To keep hope alive, leaders must inspire constituents to see positive images of the future.[19] As athletes and their coaches have known for a long time, stored mental pictures influence performance. Unless you can see yourself as being successful, it is very difficult to produce the behavior that leads to success. Experiment after experiment shows that positive images make groups more effective, relieve symptoms of illness, and enhance achievement in school, the military, and business organizations.[20]

Dutch sociologist Fred Polak backed up this observation, noting that "the rise and fall of images of the future precedes or accompanies the rise and fall of cultures. As long as a society's image is positive and flourishing, the flower of culture is in full bloom. Once the image begins to decay and lose its vitality, however, the culture does not long survive."[21] Other researchers have shown how the positive nature and frequency of stories told within an organization favorably impact motivation, commitment, and performance.[22] Given the frequently negative portrayal of businesses in the media, the growing lack of confidence in institutional leaders, and the increasing cynicism of the workforce, it's critical that you, and all leaders, begin painting more affirmative images and stories for yourself and your constituents. This requires learning to be optimistic, positive, and contagiously enthusiastic.

Positive leadership breeds positive emotions. Barbara Fredrickson, professor of psychology at the University of North Carolina at Chapel Hill, has been studying positivity for more than twenty years. Her findings indicate that a positive approach will change your life: "Positivity opens us up. The first core truth about positive emotions is that they open our hearts and our minds, making us more receptive and more creative."[23]

According to her research, positivity stretches people's minds, opens them up to new possibilities, and expands their worldview. They see more options and become more creative and innovative. It's not just wild and crazy ideas, either. When feeling positive, studies show, managers are more accurate and more careful in making decisions. They're also more interpersonally effective.[24]

Leaders who are hopeful and positive also tend to be optimistic. Optimists look at the future and see positive possibilities because of their expectation that things will work out for the best. These positive expectations motivate optimists to be proactive and to take actions that improve their work performance and their physical and mental health. In contrast, pessimists invent negative scenarios and see probabilities of failure.[25]

In fact, optimists and pessimists differ dramatically in the habitual ways they explain why events happen. Psychologist Martin Seligman and his colleagues have found that pessimists see failed events as permanent, universal, and personal defeats. They blame themselves for the bad things that happen, and they ascribe the good things to conditions not under their control. Optimists, on the other hand, tend to see defeats as temporary and having specific, not universal, causes. They blame circumstances for the bad things that happen. And when good things happen to optimists, they believe that good things always happen to them, that positive events enhance them, and that good things come from their actions and not their circumstances.[26]

Optimism is essential to strengthening credibility. Leaders with their eyes on an ideal and a positive image of the future reflect optimistic outlooks. In expressing their convictions that the future will work out for the best and be better than the past and present, optimists instill confidence in others. Constituents begin to adopt a similar attitude—and when they look to the future, they also see the possibilities of success.

Appreciating these findings, credible leaders employ a number of distinct strategies to inspire positivity and optimism. For example, when a failure or setback occurs, they don't blame themselves or the people working on the project. Instead they find situational circumstances that contributed to the failure and convey a belief that this particular situation is likely to be temporary, not permanent. They stress that the failure or setback means a problem only in this one instance and not in every case. When success occurs and milestones are reached, leaders who want to breed optimism will attribute success to the individuals in the group. They convey a belief that many more victories are at hand and they predict that good fortune will be with them for a long time.

The good news is that these qualities of hope, positivity, and optimism can be developed. Using videotaped interviews and other learning methods, researchers have been able, for example, to nurture hope in entering college freshmen and the adoption of positive health habits in women.[27] By enabling people to see the possibilities inherent in a hopeful and positive outlook they have been successful in improving performance in teaching, in learning, in sales, in nursing, in management, and in other domains of work and life.[28] Others have found that positivity can be developed through mindfulness training and meditation.[29]

None of this is to suggest that you should avoid getting people to accept personal responsibility and accountability. Optimism and personal responsibility are not mutually exclusive. People can own the problem and accept responsibility for its consequences either with an optimistic attitude that will enable them to persist in solving it, or with a pessimistic attitude that defeats them before they even start. Which person would you rather have leading your team? Which leader would you rather be? It's your choice.

While the ledger shows that organizations benefit most from optimists, don't write off the pessimists completely. They're the ones likely to ask the tough questions and probe about whether a strategy has really worked or will work. The wide-eyed optimist who believes it is possible to do anything may lead the group right into bankruptcy. People need one or two pessimists around to keep them honest, to keep them on their toes, to hold out the caution flag, and to insist that careful and critical insights be applied to problem solving.[30]

Optimism, like hope, does not mean simply waiting for good things to happen; it means acting in ways that create positive futures. But positive futures do not always come easily. Sometimes, if not always, struggles and suffering are necessary to achieve greatness. Like success in athletics, success in business is governed by the rule of "no pain, no gain." Even the hardiest of world-class competitors pull muscles, strain ligaments, tear tendons, and break bones. While no one—athlete, business leader, government official, or NGO leader—ever hopes for injury, each experiences it. And each has to work through the pain. Leaders who are not willing to personally suffer the pain and strain of Olympic-level competition will find that their credibility quickly diminishes.

Unleash Your Passion

In looking back on his experience at Morgan Stanley, Adam Carson realized that much of his success and leadership came from his "enthusiasm and passion." He explained:

> From the beginning, I had sleepless nights thinking about the
> project, but I followed that passion in order to make my dreams

165

become reality. Getting that job was the culmination of lots of persistence and hard work and definitely one of my proudest accomplishments. Looking back on the event, I truly believe that I got the job because of my passion and excitement.

I carried that passion with me whenever I walked into a room for the next few months, and the response was amazing. People were so interested in what I was teaching and talking about, not necessarily because they personally cared so much about the subject, but because they could see how deeply I cared. Being passionate enabled me to be a great leader.

Simply put, Adam said: "I am at my best when I am passionate and care deeply about what I am doing." This same sentiment is echoed by leaders everywhere—leaders such as Mindy Grossman, who said: "Take the time to absolutely find out what makes you excited to wake up in the morning."[31]

When Mindy first arrived at Home Shopping Network (HSN) as its new chief executive, she knew the environment was not positive and needed to change. HSN had had seven CEOs in the past ten years, which meant lots of changes in direction and style. As Mindy saw it, "What happens in that kind of situation is that everybody freezes"—motivation, commitment, relationships, and trust diminish. With such feelings across the organization, she realized she had to enlist others in order to impart change. Mindy said, "[I wanted to] inspire the organization to all go in the same direction. You know that you need evangelists to be able to do that, who share your passion and your vision for where you want to go."

Mindy exemplifies the principle of knowing what you are passionate about in order to be a credible leader. For her, being a leader is more than striving to maximize shareholder value or deliver on some other corporate credo. She truly respects the company and the people and derives satisfaction from seeing them work symbiotically: "It's an incredible feeling every day to come into an organization that you love, you care about, and you're helping to not just drive the business, but people's lives.... You're contributing to their growth, their development, and their talent. It is an incredible feeling." Clearly, she is passionate about the business, but also about the people who work there—and that is a formula that allowed Mindy to come in and lead a turnaround of that organization.

The other realization about passion is that suffering breeds increased passion for the goal or cause. The myth is that passion comes from joy. It does not. The word *passion* has its roots in the Greek and Latin words for suffering. The most passionate people are those who have suffered the most (recall Adam's comment, "At the beginning I had many sleepless nights"). Leaders have risked their independence, their fortunes, their health, and sometimes their lives for people and a purpose beyond themselves. Passion earned from suffering is inspiring to every constituent—from direct reports to colleagues, and very often even to the competition. John Hope Bryant explained that his passion for financial literacy was fueled by the financial setbacks he suffered early in his life and led to his founding of Operation HOPE. John said, "Just as steel is forged through fire, leaders are forged through loss. There can be no strength, no real inner growth, without the pain of legitimate suffering. It's a scientific fact: you cannot have a rainbow without a storm."[32]

Leaders who are truly inspirational are among the first to suffer. They are willing to take the first step out into the unknown, to confront self-doubt, to suffer defeat and disappointment, and return to triumph. Leaders who risk embarrassment and ruin and yet succeed in maintaining the strength of conviction give others hope. Someone who sits by in comfort while ordering others to suffer is no leader.

Suffering does not mean that leaders have to wear sackcloth and hair shirts. They need not necessarily cut their pay to zero and give up the positions they have legitimately earned through hard work, experience, and education. What is evident, however, is that leaders, especially the most senior ones, must participate in the pain like every other member of the organization. Sharing the gain means sharing the pain.

When leaders share in the pain they develop compassion for others who are suffering. *Compassion* means "to suffer *together*." Only those who have suffered with their constituents can genuinely uplift others. Only those who have felt the pain of loss and yearning for fulfillment can truly inspire. The increase in cynicism over the last several years is due in part to the perception that those in senior leadership positions have not suffered with their constituents—that they are unwilling to risk what they have gained for the sake of the cause. The perception is that they care only for themselves and care nothing for anyone else. It is ironic that those in power most risk losing everything when they are least willing to give up just a little.

Give Love and Support

Through Operation HOPE, John Hope Bryant has had the chance to meet and work with many business, political, and social leaders in his campaign to improve the financial literacy of the poor. He said of those leaders who are the most exemplary: "They all are leaders whose successes have come from caring more about others than themselves. Their power comes from love. That's why people *want* to follow them."[33]

While he's from an entirely different background, author and quality consultant Pat Townsend, a retired Marine Corps major, would agree with John. Pat wrote about leadership while in the Corps and made these observations:

> Perhaps the most obvious thing that leadership and love have in common is the act of caring about the welfare of others—an act that is central to both. One's love for another implies caring for the well-being, physical and mental, of the other. . . . A person who would call himself (or herself) a leader of Marines must be capable of love, of allowing themselves to be loved, and of understanding the awesome responsibilities incurred when one seeks and accepts the love of others. . . . The technical knowledge, the courage, the personal integrity so often discussed are definitely necessary. Love though is what makes it work; it is what makes the followers willingly accept the technical knowledge and treat the courage and personal integrity as something to emulate rather than just applaud.[34]

This sentiment about the connection between love and leadership mirrors what former publishing executive Jim Autry discusses in his book *Love and Profit: The Art of Caring Leadership*.[35] *Love* and *profit* are two words not often spoken in the same breath or seen on the same page. But when we interviewed him Jim observed, "Creating a caring workplace—a place in which people have friendships and deep personal connections and can grow personally and emotionally, psychologically, spiritually, as well as financially and professionally—is an important aspect of creating profit."

As part of creating profit, Jim recommended that you need to do more than like what you're doing. He maintains that "you should fall in love with it . . . I started really liking to be a manager, but . . . it was only after developing and evolving a way of doing things in a management style that came to be the love and profit style, the community-building style, that I could see extraordinary fruits." Indeed, in his eleven years as president the benefits he saw were impressive: the company's revenue more than tripled, and the number of magazines published grew from four to sixteen.

The loving leadership approaches of leaders fit squarely with what Yale professor Robert Sternberg (one of the foremost researchers in the fields of human intelligence and love) and his colleague Susan Grajek have found are the essential aspects of loving relationships. They report that the general factor of love "seems well identified as one of interpersonal communication, sharing and support."

> Its aspects include especially (a) deep understanding of the other, (b) sharing of ideas and information, (c) sharing of deeply personal ideas and feelings, (d) receipt and provision of emotional support to the other, (e) personal growth through the relationship and helping the other in his or her personal growth, (f) giving help to the other, (g) making the other feel needed and needing the other, and (h) the giving and receiving of affection in the relationship.[36]

While not all of these elements may be appropriate to every aspect of business, it is striking how many are integral to the six disciplines of credibility. The empirical evidence clearly demonstrates that when people believe that another person understands them, they give that person more credibility. Listening to the ideas of another person and sharing personal information about oneself also increase credibility. Developing others, helping others, increasing others' self-esteem, and expressing genuine concern for others are all behaviors of credible leaders. Could it be that giving love is the ultimate act of earning credibility?

When people can talk about what they love to do, gain a deeper understanding of others, share more intimately with others, and truly enjoy the interaction, the energy and passion that are released are contagious. By caring, loving, and showing compassion you can release a spirit in people that is unequaled. This show of encouragement is something that you can do in business every day without sentimentality or overbearing flattery.

Being supportive is how leaders sustain hope over time. They make friends, form caring relationships, and enjoy the company of others. They have a dense network of friends and colleagues whom they can call on to extend a helping hand in times of need. Credible leaders recognize how vital their sources of support are to them. They also know how essential it is to extend their support to others—and that through their support they can make a difference in people's lives.

Steve Shepstone, who was a partner in Peckham Shepstone & Associates (a U.K. outdoor education company) when we interviewed him, related an incident involving one of his most admired leaders, an incident that clearly affected him. During a very competitive rugby match, Steve's physical education teacher and rugby coach abruptly stopped the game, turned to the crowd in the stands, and shouted loudly that the tackle Shepstone had just made was the best he had ever seen. Shepstone was 5 feet 6 inches tall at the time. His opponent was 6 feet 6 inches.

That best-ever tackle had occurred decades earlier, but Steve recalled it as if it were today. He reported that when he was with this admired leader, he felt "proud, confident, and wanting to do it again." Imagine wanting to go out again and tackle someone a foot taller than you. The leader's support and recognition made that possible. When people feel supported by their leaders and appreciated for their efforts they want to go out and tackle even bigger challenges.

To encourage confidence, enliven team spirit, breed optimism, sustain hope, and foster resilience, leaders learn to look to the bright side. You must take charge of the situation and enable others to gain a sense of control over their own lives. You must demonstrate flexibility in trying a new course when the traditional approaches point to a dead end. You must talk positively about the future and selflessly share the success of achieving excellence. You must continuously seek and offer the support necessary to withstand the hardships of the struggle, and you must make the personal sacrifices needed to thrive.

Hope is an attitude in action. Hope enables people to mobilize their healing powers and their achieving powers. Hope enables them to transcend the difficulties of today and envision the potentialities of tomorrow. Hope enables people to bounce back even after being stressed, stretched, and depressed. Hope enables people to find the will and the way to aspire to greatness. Hope is testimony to the power of the human spirit.

SUSTAIN HOPE
Key Ideas From Chapter Eight

- Hope is essential to achieving the highest levels of performance.

- Constituents want leaders with a positive, confident, gritty, can-do approach who remain passionate despite obstacles and setbacks.

- To keep hope alive, credible leaders rouse optimistic feelings and enable their constituents to hold positive thoughts about the possibilities of success.

- Credible leaders balance hope with persistence and hard work.

- Credible leaders are at their best when they are passionate about what they are doing.

- Being supportive is an important way for credible leaders to sustain hope over time.

- Credible leaders create workplaces where people become friends and make deep personal connections.

- Credible leaders enable people to grow and develop themselves.

CHAPTER NINE

The Struggle to Be Human

Uncertainty is the new normal. The old order has been so shaken that it's become impossible to describe exactly what the present or the future holds. And yet, more and more people are asking, "Where are we headed? What's the vision for the future?"[1] This is the credibility conundrum of our age: given how uncertain the organizational environment is and how diverse the constituencies are, how can you achieve consensus on the values that should guide your team and organization?

In the new global marketplace, long-standing processes do not work as they once did, so organizations purge the old and wasteful ones, experimenting with bold and more intelligent systems. Trial-and-error and falling forward become the norm. Constituent heterogeneity multiplies, barriers to collaboration tumble, and functional and departmental boundaries become ambiguous. Environmental concerns collide with industrial demands.[2]

How should organizations be structured? Which values should guide organizational decision making? What impact will multinational and increasingly diverse workforces have on organizations and communities? How will a new generation of Millennials change the human dynamics in the workplace? What skills will be needed for the coming decades, and what are the educational policies necessary to help develop them? What levers need to be pulled in order to fix domestic and global economies? What will be the true impact of global interdependence on the nature of organizations? There is no consensus, only uncertainty.

Credibility is earned when you "Do What We Say We Will Do." But if the situation itself doesn't hold still long enough for you to be consistent, how can you be seen as trustworthy? If you don't know which variables will influence the outcome, how can you be seen as competent? If you have to keep experimenting with new approaches, how can you be seen as enthusiastically committed to your beliefs?

There are no easy or certain answers to questions like these. But of this you can be certain: credibility is the foundation of leadership. Act in ways that increase people's belief that you are honest, competent, inspiring, and forward-looking, and people will be much more likely to want to follow your direction. In the preceding chapters, we presented evidence and actions that will help you do this. But there are no guarantees. Perhaps we should have told you this earlier: you can perfectly execute everything that we've prescribed and still get fired!

Organizational life is full of struggles and tensions. These tensions can stretch people to their limits, and not all will be quite sure if they are up to it. Not only that, the realization is setting in that today's turmoil and global challenges will probably continue indefinitely. The world is experiencing a fundamental restructuring of economic, political, and social systems.[3] Organizations are likely to seem more like organized anarchies than like the bureaucracies that typified the public and private sectors in preceding decades.

Leaders feel these tensions acutely because of their responsibilities to set the example and inspire others to work collaboratively toward a shared vision of the future. The leaders who are the most in touch with their constituents—and therefore likely to be the most credible—will experience the pain most intensely. Let's acknowledge these tensions;

175

furthermore, let's even suggest that leaders would do well to learn to love the struggles. Where there is tension there is also energy. And where there is energy, there is also the possibility of movement. And where there is movement, there is the chance for progress. Making forward progress is the measure of leadership. So let's wrestle with three of the tensions and dilemmas that leaders experience as they stretch to strengthen credibility.

Tension Between Freedom and Constraint

Organizational consultant Neale Clapp once told us that the fundamental tension for people in organizations is the tension between freedom and constraint. When do you delegate and when do you decide? When do you accept another's authority and when do you rebel against it? When do you empower others and when do you use authority or position power? When do you set limits and when do you break the rules? When do you listen and when do you tell? When do you let go and when do you hold on?

To say that leaders should always increase freedom and relax all constraints is intellectually dishonest and totally unrealistic. To say that constituents should always accept the constraints and never challenge the status quo is equally dishonest and unrealistic. Count on people to strive to be free. Also count on organizations to exert constraints. Part of a leader's job is to engage people in grappling with the tension between freedom and constraint.

You can see this wrestling in experiments with flextime, telecommuting, in-company day care, parental leave, quality programs, and self-directed and virtual work teams. Discussions about empowerment are essentially a dialogue about freedom and constraint. Allowing more freedom is becoming the norm. But it would be foolish and irresponsible to expect organizations to abandon all constraints. Institutions must have limits; the question is not whether there should be constraints, but how many, how much, and of what type.

What does this tension between freedom and constraint have to do with strengthening credibility? Leaders demonstrate their commitment to a consistent set of expectations by clarifying meaning, unifying constituents, and intensifying actions. This process tugs at an uneasy tension between liberty and limits. Be clear about the fact that people will have choices, but be equally clear that choices are constrained. They are constrained by the owners, the shareholders, the customers, the economic system, the idiosyncrasies of the founders, the executives in power, and the people in the room at the time, along with a host of other forces, seen and unseen.

It is the leader's responsibility to make sure that everyone has the opportunity to express opinions and to get a fair hearing. Provide the forum for discussion, debate, and reconciliation. Don't ram credos through just for the sake of expediency. Values discussions should be intense. If there isn't energy and passion in the discussion, then you should be skeptical about what is being said. This doesn't mean that everyone has to pound the table, but it does mean that everyone should be able to feel the emotions when anyone in your group speaks about personal beliefs.

Leaders should not pretend that listening is the same thing as agreeing. They should not pretend that any constituent group will be able to get everything it wants. Or that people will be allowed to do their own thing, or come and go as they please. You should also not pretend the process goes on forever, and that every time a new person joins the organization you will go through the consensus-building process all over again. Timetables must be set, decisions must be made, and people must get on with it. There comes a time when the group must agree to live by certain values, at least for the foreseeable future. An organization needs to have its foundation solidly in place for a period of time in order for it to develop and grow. A constantly shifting foundation does serious structural damage to an organization. No enterprise can afford that.

What should people do if they find the team's or organization's values inconsistent with their personal values? The first responsible action is to ask for clarification: "What does this value really mean?" If there is still conflict, then manage the disagreement. Ask: "What can we do so that the organization can keep its integrity and I can keep mine?" Usually either the process of clarifying or the process of negotiating will reconcile the dilemma. If you have clarified and negotiated and conflict still exists, there are at least two other choices: withdrawal or rebellion. But if you choose the latter, do so with the understanding that the organization will deal with the rebellion as a challenge to the community and to the shared values and norms that make it whole.

The decision to sign on, get out, or rebel is an issue of personal responsibility. Personal responsibility (with its close cousin personal accountability) continues to be a hot phrase these days; managements, human resource professionals, politicians, and self-help gurus say that everyone needs more of it. But what does it really mean to be *responsible* or *accountable*?

Dictionaries, management texts, and psychology books are of little help in answering this question. If you look for *responsibility* in *The Great Ideas: A Syntopicon of Great Books of the Western World*, the index will direct you to punishment, sin, and will.[4] *Punishment. Sin. Will*. In Western philosophy, from Aeschylus and Sophocles through the Old and New Testaments to Hegel and Kant, the personal responsibility discourse has been about whether people unreservedly choose their actions or whether they are divinely predestined to act in certain ways. Hence the term *free will*. Freely choosing to do something is an indispensable condition for empowerment. Free choice is also an indispensable condition for the punishment of civil misdeeds or of religious sin.

Personal responsibility can exist only if people have free will and if they exercise it. Personal responsibility cannot exist independent of choice. In personally choosing to act, individuals are saying explicitly or implicitly, "I will accept the consequences of my actions." The credibility-strengthening process hinges upon the belief that human beings are personally accountable for their own actions. People are held accountable against the standard of shared values upon which there has been agreement. Ignoring this precept, as many leaders have in not accepting the consequences of their own actions, is exactly what contributes to increasing levels of cynicism, followed by apathy.

In setting out on a course to strengthen credibility you are embarking on an ancient philosophical quest. You are seeking to understand the powers and limitations of your humanity. The tension between freedom and constraint will be felt in every choice you make. But the overriding decision for you as for every individual is whether you are willing to take personal responsibility and to be held accountable for the path you choose.

Tension Between Leading and Following

Each individual is always a leader and a follower in the same organization at the same time, yet there are times in your career when the two collide. Take the case of a former senior vice president of marketing for a large packaged goods company. Several years ago he faced a critical leadership challenge: new technology had made it possible to introduce a substitute for his company's food product. Major customers were shifting to the food substitute. His market studies clearly indicated that the future of the industry lay in the new product. He was convinced that his company had to revise its long-range plans and develop its own entry into the market or suffer disastrous consequences.

He took his studies to the board and urged development of a market entry. The board did not share his point of view. It authorized its own independent investigations, directing two prestigious management consulting firms to determine market trends and the technical feasibility of producing the product. To the board's surprise, the consulting reports supported the senior vice president's sense of the market. Still unconvinced but now a bit worried, the board asked two law firms to determine whether entry into the new market would pose any antitrust issues. Both sets of lawyers agreed there would be no problem.

Despite the overwhelming evidence that the senior vice president's strategic vision was clear and attainable, the board sought the opinion of yet a third law firm. This one gave the board the answer it apparently was looking for all along. This third law firm thought there might be a chance of some legal hassles, so the company abandoned the pursuit of the new product. The senior vice president, however, could not in good conscience go along with the decision—to him it was a matter of integrity. He felt so strongly about his vision for the industry that he continued to pursue it. Despite an untarnished reputation and a superb track record, he could not persuade his management to undertake a new strategic direction. The board won out—and he subsequently left the organization.[5]

This critical incident illustrates how people in organizations experience this tension: *When do I lead and when do I follow?* It doesn't matter what the level, the dilemma is ever present. Part of the stress stems from the distinct differences between what people expect of leaders and what they expect of colleagues and teammates: these expectations are in dramatic conflict.

In addition to asking people to complete a checklist of the characteristics they look for and admire in a leader, we often ask them the same question about a colleague, someone they would like to work alongside as a team member on a project. Respondents select from the checklist the seven characteristics that they most looked for and admired.

The leader-colleague comparisons reflect some extremely important similarities—and some significant differences. The expectations of U.S. leaders and colleagues are set forth in Table 9.1, with characteristics listed in rank order.

TABLE 9.1 The Characteristics Desired in Leaders and Colleagues

For Leaders	Percentage of People Selecting Characteristic	For Colleagues	Percentage of People Selecting Characteristic
Honest	85	Honest	82
Forward-looking	70	Cooperative	71
Inspiring	69	Dependable	71
Competent	64	Competent	70
Intelligent	42	Intelligent	46
Broad-minded	40	Supportive	43
Dependable	37	Straightforward	37
Supportive	36	Broad-minded	35
Fair-Minded	35	Imaginative	32
Straightforward	31	Inspiring	31
Determined	28	Forward-looking	27
Cooperative	26	Fair-minded	25
Ambitious	26	Ambitious	20
Courageous	21	Caring	19
Caring	20	Determined	19
Loyal	18	Independent	19
Imaginative	18	Loyal	16
Mature	16	Courageous	14
Self-Controlled	11	Mature	13
Independent	6	Self-Controlled	7

In virtually every survey administration, people rank honest first on all lists. Competent also receives votes from a majority of respondents. Honest and competent, you will recall, are two of the most important elements of source credibility. People want to know that their colleagues as well as their leaders are worthy of their trust. This finding reinforces the importance of credibility in every working relationship. Whether the person is in the role of a team member, a constituent, or a leader, people need to believe in that individual.

Notice also the striking differences in these two lists. The contrasts between what people desire in a leader and what they desire in a colleague help to better understand one of the basic dilemmas facing any person who would be a leader—the tension between when to assent and when to dissent, between when to join and when to part, when to cooperate and when to initiate.

It's been noted that people expect their leaders to be forward-looking—to have a sense of direction and a concern for the future of the organization. People also expect leaders to be inspiring—to be enthusiastic, energetic, and positive about the future. Leaders must be able to communicate their visions in ways that uplift and encourage people to enlist. In combination, forward-looking and inspiring make a leader visionary and dynamic. They make a person magnetic and attractive to others. They point people in new, pioneering directions and give them energy and drive. They get people focused on and enthusiastic about building the organization of the future, putting today's actions in a strategic context. Add to this the rest of the foundation of credibility—honest and competent—and you would think you would have an unbeatable formula for success.

But look again. The qualities of forwarding-looking and inspiring are conspicuously absent from the top of the list of what people most want from their colleagues. Instead people preferred that colleagues be dependable and cooperative. People want to know that they can count on their colleagues to be responsible team players. They want to know everyone can work together collaboratively and will subordinate individual needs to group goals.

Having dependable and cooperative colleagues is absolutely essential to accomplishing even the most mundane tasks in organizations. People must be able to rely on each other, to get along with each other, and to set aside personal agendas for the good of the organization. Without dependability and cooperation, no group task would ever get done, and politics would be rampant.

But here's the rub. Being forward-looking and inspiring is often not harmonious with being cooperative and dependable. Let's say that you envision a new product or service that will take the organization in new directions. You have done your homework, and you are convinced that the market is going to demand what you envision. Meanwhile, your team has invested time, energy, even careers in pursuing the current strategic vision of the organization. You are listened to politely but then told to get back to getting the gang fired up about the existing plan. Yet your personal integrity and your energy will not allow you to just forget it, so you persist. You sell even harder. Pretty soon people start to wonder what happened to the loyal team player. Why aren't you getting on board? Why aren't you cooperating? Despite pleadings for more effective leadership, there are times when people would be just as pleased to have a better team player.

The norms of cooperativeness and dependability, as essential as they are to teamwork, can also inhibit organizational change and growth. Too rigidly adhered to, they can result in faithful allegiance to the status quo and unquestioning loyalty to the party line. They can also impede the development of the leadership skills so needed in organizations today.

If your vision of the future is not in alignment with that of your hierarchical superiors or your teammates, you may be perceived as uncooperative and disloyal *even if your view is correct*. Persistently selling a point of view may only reinforce this perception and may diminish the support of colleagues and managers alike. It may lead to being branded a renegade. It may even get you fired, transferred, or asked to "voluntarily" depart.

There is a crucial difference between a pioneering leader and a dependable colleague. While success in both is founded on personal credibility, leadership requires the realization of a unique and ideal image of the future. Teamwork requires cooperation and reliable adherence to that common vision. Leadership and teamwork are certainly not mutually exclusive—in fact, exemplary leaders foster collaboration—yet there is a dynamic tension between them. Sometimes when an individual's vision is in conflict with the existing strategic vision of an organization, a choice is demanded: Do I lead or do I follow? Do I work with the group in the direction we've agreed or do I set off on a new course?

There is no easy path to take. If individuals cannot learn to subordinate themselves to a shared purpose, then no one will follow and selfishness and anarchy will rule. Yet to grow and improve, organizations must create a climate that fosters leadership; they must encourage the honest articulation of fresh strategic visions of the future.

In these uncertain times it is absolutely necessary for leaders to encourage and tolerate more internal conflict than has been allowed in the past. If organizations expect people to show initiative in meeting today's serious business challenges, then they have to relax their expectations of abiding devotion. Instead, they must support efforts of honest and competent people to find solutions to the problems that are confronting their companies. In short, they must develop the leader in everyone.

Tension Between Definitions of Success

What's the criterion for leadership success? Is success defined only in terms of the scale and scope of influence? Is the ultimate objective of leaders to have the largest number of constituents? Are leaders successful only if they can spread their influence beyond the plant or department to the company? Or beyond the company to the country? Or even beyond the country to an international audience? Is it possible to be judged a credible and successful leader if you guide only 12 people to places they have never been before? Or must it be 120, 1,200, 12,000, 120,000, or 1,200,000? Is it the responsibility of successful leaders to enlist ever greater numbers of constituents in their vision and values? Can leaders be said to be extraordinarily successful if they choose to lead a small organization for their entire careers, or even a single team or department?

What of the neighbor who organizes a local fundraising drive for the homeless, or the line employee who starts the company's recycling program, or the student who starts a campaign to get kids off drugs, or the woman who opens a small shop in the Grand Bazaar? Are these people leaders? Is the leadership label reserved only for people in exalted or hierarchical positions?

The measure of scale pervades a lot of discussions about success. The more constituents you have, the better at leading you must be goes one line of reasoning. This argument is easy to understand. It takes extraordinary talent and energy to lead a large company, country, or movement, particularly over time. Outstanding skills are necessary. Certainly there is a level of superior competence involved.

But taken to its logical extreme, with this definition no leader could ever be judged successful, even those who have influenced millions. Judaism, Islam, Buddhism, Hinduism, and Christianity, for example, have thrived for centuries. Moses, Mohammed, Siddhartha Gautama, Ramanuja, Confucius, and Jesus Christ are considered by many to be extraordinary leaders. But in their lifetimes not one converted every soul to his religion. Not everyone has been converted to this day.

Or take another person on the list of most-admired leaders, Mother Teresa. Her ceaseless compassionate work on behalf of the poor around the world won her a Nobel Prize, and following her death she was beatified by Pope John Paul II and given the title Blessed Teresa of Calcutta. Yet she had very few constituents by comparison to many corporate chief executive officers. Does that mean she was not as good a leader?

And what about Mikhail Gorbachev? The changes in the former Soviet Union brought about during his tenure were not even imaginable prior to his assumption of the leadership role. Yet he failed to retain the support of his constituents and was replaced. Was Gorbachev, therefore, not a credible leader? In a similar vein, do the problems facing South Africa today deny the leadership effectiveness of Nelson Mandela?

To judge leadership effectiveness on the basis of scale, scope, and time is ultimately to limit to a very few the potential number of people who can lead. If converting or enlisting everyone were the criterion for success, it would be said that there have never been any leaders. No one has ever enlisted 100 percent of the potential constituents in anything. People often ask a related question about the leaders mentioned in books like this one. "What happened after they left?" "Is the organization, product, or program still operating by the same principles, or was it only possible when their sponsor was there?" If the organization operated by one set of principles only while you were the plant manager, superintendent, or program or project manager and then adopted some new ones when a new leader arrived, would that make you less of a leader? And what does that say about the willingness to allow others the opportunity to make their unique contributions? If the new leader made significant changes, would that necessarily negate what the previous leader had accomplished?

These issues of scope, scale, and time reflect one's values. If you value bigger, grander, longer then you are likely to be disappointed in most leaders and in yourself. Leadership is both local and global. Acts of credible leadership come in all sizes. You can lead people to change the world, the state, the community, the workplace, the neighborhood, and the family. Or, you can just lead yourself to change. Leadership is also transitory and most often lasts a relatively short time. There are those whose influence has spanned centuries and crossed continents, but they are not the only ones who have led. Those whose influence has spanned only a few days and a few blocks can still have taken people to places they have never been before.

So what defines success? When it comes to leadership, perhaps the most appropriate response is the one adopted by such organizations as the Scouts and the Sierra Club. Whether your leadership is confined to your own 25 square feet or extends to the plant's 250,000 square feet or to the corporation's 2,500,000 square feet, success is leaving the place better than you found it.

From Excellence to Excess

The six disciplines of credibility are a means for building the foundation of leadership, and there's strong evidence to back this framework up. Methods and techniques are available for everyone to use in achieving mastery and excellence in the fundamentals of leader-constituent relations. Excellence is a noble goal. To be preeminent in one's profession is a worthy pursuit. To surpass the average and to become superior is what makes for high-quality services and products. But one can go too far. One can go beyond excellence to excess. This isn't about an excess

187

of excellence, but an *excessive* focus on each credibility discipline for the sake of perfecting the method instead of producing the intended result. Excessive focus on the disciplines can mean the unfortunate triumph of technique over purpose.

It may be hard to imagine how you can have too much self-knowledge or too much appreciation or too much affirmation or too much mastery or too much service or too much hope. But you can indulge in each of the credibility disciplines to extremes beyond what is necessary and sufficient and end up with negative characteristics that can damage credibility. The line between excellence and excess is often a fine one. Consider these caution signs to watch for on your leadership credibility journey and bear in mind the antidotes for overindulgence in any of the disciplines, as summarized in Table 9.2

TABLE 9.2 From Excellence to Excess

Discipline	Excess Leads to	Antidote Required
Discovering Your Self	Arrogance	Openness
Appreciating Constituents	Fragmentation	Complexity
Affirming Shared Values	Rigidity	Challenge
Developing Capacity	Vanity	Humility
Serving a Purpose	Subservience	Independence
Sustaining Hope	Dependence	Action

From Self-Discovery to Arrogance

Discovery of self and self-knowledge are essential to building leader credibility. People do not trust someone who is not clear about personal beliefs and who continues to shift from position to position based upon the latest opinion poll. But you must watch out for those who are so persuaded that their values are the right values that they become moralistic, pious, judgmental, arrogant, or self-righteous. People like this become overbearing and boorish. They are not interesting to other people, because they themselves are not interested in other people. You do not want to be around them, much less follow them.

Overconfidence is another danger of excessive self-knowledge. Critical as it is that you believe in your abilities to succeed, you risk becoming blind to the limits of your competencies. This is especially true when the environment changes and the skills that worked for you before may not continue to serve you well. Overconfidence can lead to cockiness, poor judgment, and insensitivity to the situation or to other people.

The antidote to arrogance is openness. When leaders stay open to others they avoid the hubris that sometimes comes from being in charge. Trust is maintained when people see that you are not a know-it-all and are interested in learning from others. It is also maintained when others see that you are willing to admit your own mistakes and learn from them, instead of dismissing them as someone else's problem.

From Appreciation to Fragmentation

There is ample evidence that diversity is good for business. It increases innovation. It increases the probability that decisions will reflect the broadest constituency. It increases the chances of success in a multinational marketplace with a multicultural workforce. But in the process of coming to appreciate and prize the diverse values of others, leaders must guard against vacillation and fragmentation. There may be so many constituent groups and their points of view so divergent that leaders may oscillate between one significant need and another. Or they may overpromise every group.

189

Credible leaders promote choice and do not dictate values, yet coming to a decision that motivates the largest possible constituency appears increasingly difficult. The diversity of interests makes decision making extraordinarily taxing. By honoring too many differences, leaders may create false hopes or resentment. By encouraging all voices to speak, leaders may create a Tower of Babel that can be understood by no one. There has to come a point when attending stops and choosing starts.

Most people tend to view problems and events through a very narrow frame. The everyday term *simple-minded* indicates a commonsense understanding of this phenomenon. Research suggests, however, that people who are more cognitively complex—who are able to see and understand their environments from several different perspectives—are more effective. They are more tolerant of ambiguity, less prejudiced, better able to resolve conflicts cooperatively, and better able to make moral judgments.[6]

The antidote to fragmentation is complexity. The ability to take a 360-degree view will help you to know that your decision is credible, even if a powerful constituency may not agree with it. Diversity complicates a leader's job, but those who can handle the complexity make better leaders.

From Affirmation to Rigidity

Our research indicates that shared values make a difference to the leader, to constituents, and to the organization. A leader must build consensus around core beliefs and then publicly affirm what has been agreed. Leaders find common ground, they build a sense of community, and they resolve dilemmas on the basis of principles and not hierarchical positions. Shared values are an attribute of a strong organizational culture. Strong cultures can produce strong performance.

However, shared values can become straitjackets. A shared value that was once a cornerstone of the organizational foundation can become obsolete. Rigid adherence to cultural norms can hurt long-term performance. A strong culture can easily result in arrogance—and in an inward focus that results in organizational politics and dysfunctional bureaucratic processes. In today's rapidly changing world, these characteristics undermine performance.

Consensus on norms and values also makes people subject to groupthink. The strong desire to maintain harmony and cohesion among group members, and an understandable need to maintain their own self-esteem, inclines people to avoid creating discord. They choose not to bring up contrary points of view, and they censor themselves from raising doubts about a policy decision. The results can be disastrous.[7]

Moreover, communities can become cults, limiting free choice and rewarding only blind obedience. The conformance can be deadly, as in the case of the mass suicides at Jonestown (Guyana), or simply numbing. Communities can also become country clubs, emphasizing the needs of the members over the needs of the larger constituencies, such as customers and shareholders. This country-club norm can quickly cause a group to become irrelevant and out of touch with the outside world.

The antidote to rigidity is challenge. To keep the organization from becoming stiff and inflexible, leaders must consciously induce a challenge to the established values. They should take a periodic look at their values to see if they are still legitimate—and if not, to determine what to do about it.

191

From Development to Vanity

Credible leaders develop the capacity of people to deliver on their shared values. They give people choices and latitude; they educate and build confidence. In the credible organization, everyone is a leader; all are masters of their own fate.

Yet excessive development can lead to vanity. It can lead to the leadership and organizational equivalents of the posers on Muscle Beach who strut around flexing their biceps. Their sole purpose is to look good, not to be healthy. The right cars, the right carpets, the right paintings, the right clothes, the right restaurants, the right clubs, the right gadgets, the right trophies become more important than doing the right thing. As the late psychologist George Leonard, author of thirteen books and holder of a third-degree aikido black belt, pointed out, "If you're always thinking about appearances, you can never attain the state of concentration that's necessary for effective learning and top performance."[8]

Excessive self-improvement can lead to a continuous striving for perfection. Mastery experiences are essential to developing confidence, but as George explained, "Mastery is not about perfection. It's about a process, a journey. The master is the one who stays on the path, day after day, year after year. The master is the one who is willing to try, and fail, and try again, for as long as he or she lives."[9]

Perfectionism makes people continuously dissatisfied with their own performances and those of others. It causes them to interfere with the learning of others and to become intolerant of mistakes. Perfectionists never let others shine in their own way. Leaders who strive for perfection are likely to become tyrants. Vanity and perfectionism contribute to an arrogance that can ultimately be the undoing of excellent companies and of excellent leaders.

Excessive emphasis on individual mastery can also lead to valuing personal control over organizational purpose. If everyone is master, where are the servant leaders? By developing everyone to be leaders, you are likely to increase the tension between freedom and constraint, between the rights of the individuals and the common purpose of the institution. You should always keep in mind that everyone being a leader should also mean everyone being a servant as well.

The antidote to vanity is humility. Leaders need to be aware of their own and their organization's shortcomings and be willing to admit to them. They need to encourage and support others in admitting they are wrong without fear of punishment or reprisal. People from humble organizations are proud, yet they do not allow pride to consume them. They admit, acknowledge, and apologize for mistakes.

From Serving to Subservience

Leaders serve a purpose and the people who have made it possible for them to lead. The credible leader is a servant leader, one who puts the purposes and principles of the organization ahead of all else. To remain credible as servants, leaders must stay in touch. They must go first and not ask anyone to do anything they are unwilling to do. Leaders ask questions, keep promises, hold themselves accountable, and atone for their mistakes.

But emphasizing the servant nature of leadership raises a fundamental question: When do you respond to your constituents, and when do you act on your own principles? Leaders are often faced with having to subordinate their self-interest for the common good. But there is an important distinction between subordinating and losing one's self.

Listening is important to earning credibility, and so is taking a stand. You have to acknowledge the tension. Leaders have to listen to those whom they serve. But not everyone will be in agreement, and decisions must still be made. Too much listening and too much polling of people's opinions can turn to inconsistency; it can become just trying to please, not trying to lead. There is nothing inherently contradictory about being a "servant leader" and acting on one's own beliefs. Leaders serve others when they respond to their constituents' expectation that they have a vision of the future. While it is true that credibility is the foundation of leadership, you can't ignore the one factor that differentiates leaders from other credible people—and that's being forward-looking. A clear sense of direction is something constituents want and expect from a credible leader. Being of service to others means being proactive on behalf of your constituents, and very often that means anticipating their needs or the needs of their organizations. This ability to anticipate and commit to the future is the real test of leadership.

To say that leaders must take a stand is not to suggest that the leader is always right and the constituents are always wrong. It is only to acknowledge that it is too simple to say *serve others* and everything will magically be in harmony. The process is more complex. Sometimes you should listen to your conscience instead of to your constituents. To have integrity as a leader—to be at one with the person you are in your private heart and in public places—you have to be true to yourself. Integrity demands that you vote your conscience. As long as your overall credit rating remains high, if you are occasionally a step or two ahead of your constituents on some issues, they will still give you the loan. But if your credit is all used up, and you vote only your own convictions and not theirs, they are very likely to call in the vote.

The antidote to subservience is independence. To counteract the effects of losing one's self to the cause, leaders must forge their own identities outside of the organizations they lead. You need to find something that defines you besides your work. The most expressive and successful leaders are those who take their self-knowledge and apply it to something other than their constituents. They have an abiding outside interest in which they participate actively: they sail, play the piano, perform in plays, or write poetry, as a few examples. To serve others, you must also look after yourself.

From Sustaining to Dependence

Credible leaders look on the bright side. They are optimistic and full of hope. Credible leaders go forth with love and courage. They arouse positive images and cause positive action. Credible leaders inspire others with their willingness to suffer first. They seek and give support and recognition that enables others to excel.

But too much optimism and positivity can lead to dependence on the leader's energy and enthusiasm to move things forward. It can lead to overreliance on the leader instead of self-reliance on the part of the constituents. Too much optimism can also lead to false hopes, and it can mislead others. Excessive confidence is inappropriate as an initial response if the risks are too high, if the future is dim, or if a person is in need of sympathy. Being overly upbeat and positive can blind people to the realities and to the risks; if promises are not fulfilled, people will be disillusioned and less willing to grant credit in the future. So a leader needs to define reality.

Too much supportiveness can also foster dependency. If you want self-reliant, self-directed constituencies, you can't be expected to offer support and comfort all the time. No one can be expected to be available twenty-four hours a day and still maintain personal health and worth to the organization.

Recognition and pay are often billed as motivators. But formal and informal recognition lose their power to motivate if given all the time for

195

everything. And pay is indiscriminate: it covers everything one does, well and poorly. People must be able to tell which behaviors contribute to the organization's goals and which do not. Raises and recognition must be earned, rather than expected; an entitlement mentality can deaden performance just as easily as the absence of respect and recognition can.

The antidote to dependence is action. To retain freedom, constituents must maintain faith in their will and capacity to act. If people feel helpless and victimized and believe they don't matter, they may become dependent on the leader for hope and support, surrendering themselves to this. Leaders must be alert that neither they nor their constituents make the leadership relationship a substitute for the self.

Initiate Renewal: New Beginnings from the Old Ending

People run down. Energy runs out. Talent gets stale. Organizations get stuck. Challenges continue and threats mount, and the old ways of doing things don't work anymore. If you persist in operating by the rules of the past, you can't hope to have new visions of the future. If fear and anxiety grip the workforce, action is strangled. The forward movement that defines the very nature of leadership comes to a halt.

Leaders and constituencies must first acknowledge that what once worked may not work any longer, and then they must be able to enter into a zone of uncertainty that is at first frightening but from which they emerge reenergized and renewed. In nearly every "personal best leadership" case study, leaders admit, as Fatih Mutluel did in his own situation at the Bosch Diesel Injection Factory (Bursa, Turkey), to being "both frightened and excited at the beginning." Or as Justin Brocato, marketing operations manager at Cisco Systems, explained: "I was nervous but still confident." It is admittedly scary to do something that has never been done before, and at the same time it is incredibly exhilarating to take the first step forward. Without that step, people, organizations, and communities are overtaken by the chaos of decline and decay.

Learning fuels the engine of renewal. Or, more accurately, unlearning and then learning anew. Nearly four decades ago the late Donald N. Michael, professor of planning and public policy at the University of Michigan, defined the characteristics of the new competence of learning for changing times. His observations are perhaps even more relevant today:

> I think *we have no choice* but to try to be competent in ways that are appropriate for coping with systemic turbulence, complexity, and ambiguity. This means that as persons seeking meaning in our lives, worthiness in our efforts, we have no choice but to take the risks, and accept the pain, the excitement, and the exhilaration of *becoming learners.*[10]

Don asserted that people must find it rewarding to become learners if they are going to change toward an organization that is future-responsive rather than past-reactive. These are his characteristics of the new learning competence:[11]

- Acknowledging very high levels of uncertainty and learning to live with the stress of unstable situations
- Embracing error and using mistakes as learning opportunities
- Accepting responsibility for the future and evaluating the present in the light of anticipated futures
- Developing interpersonal competence so we can learn from others
- Knowing oneself
- Creating support groups for oneself

As you look back over the cases of leaders who earned the respect of their constituents, Don's description of a learner is an apt characterization of each. They acknowledged and shared that they did not have all the answers, that they were not always in control, that they were vulnerable. In so doing they embraced their mistakes and asked what could be learned from them. They looked ahead and wondered what the world would be like in the future, especially if the visions they held were enacted. And they wrestled with the value issues revealed by their future explorations. They were highly skilled interpersonally, always asking questions and listening to advice. They knew their values and beliefs, their strengths and weaknesses. And they all had broad networks of support.

The late John Gardner asserted in his book *On Leadership* that learning and renewal are essential to all people. And leaders, he believed, have a special responsibility to renew their institutions. As John explained:

> The pace of change is swift. Institutions that have lost their capacity to adapt pay a heavy price. Yet the impulse of most leaders is much the same as it was a thousand years ago: accept the system as it is and lead it. That is rarely possible any longer. Continuous renewal is necessary. Leaders must understand how and why human systems age, and must know how the processes of renewal may be set in motion.[12]

John's advice to leaders who wish to set renewal in motion is this: "The consideration leaders must never forget is that the key to renewal is the release of human energy and talent."[13]

And so we conclude where we started our discussion of the six disciplines of credibility. Credible leaders, we said, must first discover what motivates them, what guides them, and what gives them the energy to dedicate themselves to leading. Credible leaders must also learn to appreciate what releases energy in others. But from time to time human energy runs down and talent needs to be refreshed. Renewal is required to sustain that energy. The same is true of credibility. It must be continuously renewed.

Renewing credibility is a continuous human struggle and the ultimate leadership struggle. Strenuous effort is required to build and strengthen the foundations of working relationships. Constituents do not owe leaders allegiance. Leaders earn it. The gift of another's trust and confidence is well worth the struggle and essential to meeting the challenges of leading people to places they have never been before.

THE STRUGGLE TO BE HUMAN
Key Ideas From Chapter Nine

- Uncertainty is the new normal, and uncertainty makes building and sustaining credibility even more imperative.

- Credible leaders must wrestle with the tensions that characterize organizational life today: the tension between freedom and constraint, the tension between leading and following, and the tension between the various definitions of success.

- Excessive focus on a discipline for the sake of perfecting the method thwarts its purpose and prevents the intended result.

- Self-discovery taken to excess leads to arrogance; the antidote is openness.

- Excessive appreciation of diversity leads to fragmentation; the antidote is complexity.

- Affirmation of shared values taken to the extreme leads to rigidity; the antidote is challenge.

- Excessive development of capacity, competence, and confidence can lead to vanity; the antidote is humility.

- Excessive emphasis on service leads to subservience; the antidote is independence.

- Excessive emphasis on sustaining hope leads to dependence; the antidote is action.

- Building and sustaining credibility ultimately means being a perpetual learner, with all the turmoil, stress, pain, and excitement that involves.

Character Counts

The more we study leadership, the more we're persuaded that leadership development is not simply about skill development. It's also about character development. Consider what one sage wrote:

> Be careful of your thoughts, for your thoughts become your words;
> Be careful of your words, for your words become your deeds;
> Be careful of your deeds, for your deeds become your habits;
> Be careful of your habits, for your habits become your character;
> Be careful of your character, for your character becomes your destiny.[1]

And we would humbly add:

> Be careful of your leadership, for your leadership becomes your legacy.

Read these six simple lines at the start of every day. They will remind you that what you do as a leader begins in your mind, gets expressed in your words, and then gets translated into your actions. Over time those actions become who you are, determine the credibility you earn, and shape the legacy you leave.

NOTES

Introduction: On Credibility and the Restoration of Trust and Confidence

1. J. M. Kouzes and B. Z. Posner, *Credibility: How Leaders Gain and Lose It, Why People Demand It*, 1st ed. (San Francisco: Jossey-Bass, 1993), p. 34.

2. For example, see P. Paxton and J. A. Smith, "America's Trust Fall," *Greater Good Magazine*, Fall 2008, pp. 14–17, accessed online at http://greatergood.berkeley.edu/article/item/americas_trust_fall on July 23, 2010. Also see D. Jacobe, "America's Confidence in Banks Not Improving," Gallup, July 23, 2010, accessed online at www.gallup.com/poll/141545/Americans-Confidence-Banks-Not-Improving.aspx?version =print on July 23, 2010; L. Saad, "Congress Ranks Last in Confidence in Institutions," Gallup, July 22, 2010, accessed online at www.gallup.com/poll/141512/Congress-Ranks-Last-Confidence-Institutions.aspx?version=print on July 23, 2010; "Very Few Americans Find Statements by Financial Institutions Completely Believable," Harris Interactive, May 18, 2010, accessed online at www.harrisinteractive.com/News Room/HarrisPolls/tabid/447/mid/1508/articleId/384/ctl/ReadCustom% 20Default/Default.aspx on July 23, 2010; and "Many Europeans, Especially in Britain, Have Lost Confidence in Their Elected Representatives," Harris Interactive, June 17, 2009, accessed online at

www.harrisinteractive.com/vault/HI_FinancialTimes_Harris_Poll_June_
2009_17.pdf on July 23, 2010.

3. For example, see Paxton and Smith, "America's Trust Fall."

4. For example, see Paxton and Smith, "America's Trust Fall." Also see S.
M. Lipset and W. Schneider, *The Confidence Gap: Business, Labor and
Government in the Public Mind* (New York: Free Press, 1987), p. 399.

5. If you are interested in learning more about this research, please visit our
website, www.leadershipchallenge.com/go/credibility.

6. B. Z. Posner, J. M. Kouzes, and W. H. Schmidt, "Shared Values Make
a Difference: An Empirical Test of Corporate Culture," *Human Resource
Management*, 1985, *24*(3), 293–305; B. Z. Posner, "Person-Organization
Values Congruence: No Support for Individual Differences as a Moderating Influence," *Human Relations*, 1992, *45*(4), 351–361; B. Z. Posner
and R. I. Westwood, "A Cross-Cultural Investigation of the Shared Values
Relationship," *International Journal of Value-Based Management*, 1995,
8(2), 1–10; and B. Z. Posner, "Another Look at the Impact of Personal
and Organizational Values Congruency," *Journal of Business Ethics*, 2010,
97(4), 535–541.

Chapter One: Leadership Is a Relationship

1. All of the stories told about individuals in this book are from real people.
Their titles and positions are accurate as of the time that we interacted
with them; of course, many have moved on from these positions, and
organizations have changed as well over the years. In some instances,
people preferred that we not use their names in an illustration, and we
honored this request. We have respectfully noted in the text when we
know that the individual has subsequently died.

2. J. W. Gardner, *On Leadership* (New York: Free Press, 1990),
pp. 28–29.

3. W. H. Schmidt and B. Z. Posner, *Managerial Values and Expectations:
The Silent Power in Personal and Organizational Life* (New York: Amer-
ican Management Association, 1982). Also see B. Z. Posner, J. M.
Kouzes, and W. H. Schmidt, "Shared Values Make a Difference: An

Empirical Test of Corporate Culture," *Human Resource Management*, 1985, *24*(3), 293–309; B. Z. Posner and W. H. Schmidt, "Values and the American Manager: An Update," *California Management Review*, 1984, *26*(3), 202–216; and B. Z. Posner, "Values and the American Manager: A Three-Decade Perspective," *Journal of Business Ethics*, 2010, *91*(4),457–465.

4. B. Z. Posner and W. H. Schmidt, "Values and Expectations of Federal Service Executives," *Public Administration Review*, 1986, *46*(5), 447–454.

5. We direct the attention of those who would like to know about the original empirical studies to our website, www.leadershipchallenge .com/WileyCDA/Section/id-131060.html.

6. This example was provided by Cristian Nunez in his "most admired leader" essay.

7. J. M. Kouzes and B. Z. Posner, *The Leadership Challenge,* 4th ed. (San Francisco: Jossey-Bass, 2007).

8. Only one characteristic has changed by more than 15 percentage points (plus or minus) from the first to the most current iteration of the data collection, and this is the leader characteristic of *imaginative*. In 1987 it was selected by about one-third (34 percent) of the respondents (ranked #8) and more recently only by about 18 percent (ranked #16). While creativity, innovation, and risk-taking are always important, it may be that as the overall sense of uncertainty and turmoil in the world has increased over these past thirty years, most people now look, paradoxically as it may seem, for stability and a solid foundation from their leaders rather than a widely experimental approach.

9. See, for example, D. K. Berlo, J. B. Lemert, and R. J. Mertz, "Dimensions for Evaluating the Acceptability of Message Sources," *Public Opinion Quarterly*, 1969, *33*, 563–576.

10. "Transcript: Gen. Petraeus on Staying Strong Through 'Horrific News,'" *Washington Post*, transcript of video interview by David Ignatius, February 9, 2010, accessed online at http://views.washingtonpost.com/ leadership/panelists/2010/02/transcript-gen-petraeus.html on June 3, 2010.

Chapter Two: Credibility Makes a Difference

1. See J. M. Kouzes and B. Z. Posner, *The Leadership Challenge*, 4th ed. (San Francisco: Jossey-Bass, 2007), pp. 199–211, for a discussion about how people learn to lead.
2. I. Federman, remarks to the Leavey School of Business, Santa Clara University, April 2, 1991.
3. You can find a summary of our own empirical studies on our website, www.leadershipchallenge.com/WileyCDA/Section/id-131060.html.
4. Our research built upon earlier work by Stanford University professor Charles O'Reilly, and most specifically, C. A. O'Reilly, "Charisma as Communication: The Impact of Top Management Credibility and Philosophy on Employee Involvement," paper presented to the Annual Meeting of the Academy of Management, Boston, August 1984.
5. S. M. Lipset and W. Schneider, *The Confidence Gap: Business, Labor and Government in the Public Mind* (New York: Free Press, 1987), p. 177.
6. For a discussion of management derailment, see J. Hogan, R. Hogan, and R. Kaiser, "Management Derailment: Personal Assessment and Mitigation," Hogan Assessment Systems, 2008, accessed online at www.hoganassessments.com/_hoganweb/documents/Management_Derailment.pdf on July 24, 2010. See also M. W. McCall Jr. and M. M. Lombardo, *Off the Track: Why and How Successful Executives Get Derailed*, Technical Report No. 21 (Greensboro, NC: Center for Creative Leadership, 1983); and R. E. Kaplan with W. H. Drath and J. R. Kofodimos, *Beyond Ambition: How Driven Managers Can Lead Better and Live Better* (San Francisco: Jossey-Bass, 1991).
7. McCall and Lombardo, *Off the Track*.

Chapter Three: Discover Your Self

1. As quoted in P. Jordan (producer), *The Credibility Factor* (video), in J. M. Kouzes and B. Z. Posner, Legacy: The Leadership Challenge 20th Anniversary DVD Collection (San Francisco: Pfeiffer, 2007).

2. W. Durant, *The Life of Greece* (New York: Simon & Schuster, 1939, 1966), p. 198.

3. This example comes from Shankar Ramachandran's "most admired leader" essay.

4. W. Bennis, *On Becoming a Leader*, 4th ed. (Philadelphia: Basic Books, 2009), p. 51.

5. Bennis, *On Becoming a Leader*, p. 40.

6. What we have learned from our studies of primarily business enterprises has also been found to be true in other organizations. For a look at the important role that values, capabilities, and confidence play in military leadership, see E. Jacques and S. D. Clement, *Executive Leadership: A Practical Guide to Managing Complexity* (Arlington, VA: Cason Hall, 1991), p. 31.

7. M. Rokeach, *The Nature of Human Values* (New York: Free Press, 1973), p. 5.

8. Rokeach, *The Nature of Human Values*, pp. 14–15.

9. Extensive descriptions of values clarification exercises are contained in S. B. Simon, *Values Clarification: The Classic Guide to Discovering Your Truest Feelings, Beliefs, and Goals*, rev. ed. (New York: Grand Central, 1995). For a treatment of this issue in education see T. Lickona, *Educating for Character: How Our Schools Can Teach Respect and Responsibility* (New York: Bantam Books, 1992). You might also find this tool useful: J. M. Kouzes and B. Z. Posner with J. Bell and R. Harness, *The Leadership Challenge Values Cards Facilitator's Guide* (San Francisco: Pfeiffer, 2010).

10. You will find a very interesting collection of personal credos in J. Allison and D. Gediman, *This I Believe: The Personal Philosophies of Remarkable Men and Women* (New York: Henry Holt, 2007); and J. Allison and D. Gediman, *This I Believe II: More Personal Philosophies of Remarkable Men and Women* (New York: Henry Holt, 2008). You can view some of the essays online and also contribute your own story at http://thisibelieve.org. There's even an app for your iPhone.

11. B. Z. Posner, "Values and the American Manager: A Three-Decade Perspective," *Journal of Business Ethics*, 2010, *91*(4), 457–465.

12. W. G. Scott and D. K. Hart, *Organizational Values in America* (New Brunswick, NJ: Transaction, 1990), pp. 190–191.

13. J. M. Burns, *Leadership* (New York: HarperCollins, 1978), p. 36.

14. A. Colby, L. Kohlberg, E. Speicher-Dubin, and M. Lieberman, "Secondary School Moral Discussion Programs Led by Social Studies Teachers," *Journal of Moral Education*, 1977, *6*(2), 90–111. See also Lickona, *Educating for Character*, pp. 228–248.

15. B. Z. Posner, "Individual's Moral Judgment and Its Impact on Group Processes," *International Journal of Management*, 1986, *3*(2), 5–11.

16. D. S. DeRue and N. Wellman, "Developing Leader via Experience: The Role of Developmental Challenge, Learning Orientation, and Feedback Availability," *Journal of Applied Psychology*, 2009, *94*(4), 859–875.

17. D. H. Maister, "How's Your Asset?" (Boston: David Maister Associates, 1991), p. 1.

18. Maister, "How's Your Asset?" p. 2.

19. Maister, "How's Your Asset?" p. 3.

20. Maister, "How's Your Asset?" p. 3.

21. J. M. Kouzes and B. Z. Posner, *The Truth About Leadership* (San Francisco: Jossey-Bass, 2010).

22. A. Bandura, "Conclusion: Reflections on Nonability Determinants of Competence," in *Competence Considered*, edited by R. Sternberg and J. Kolligian Jr. (New Haven, CT: Yale University Press, 1990), p. 316.

23. Bandura, "Conclusion," p. 315.

24. Bandura, "Conclusion," p. 323. See also M. E. Gist and T. R. Mitchell, "Self-Efficacy: A Theoretical Analysis of Its Determinants and Malleability," *Academy of Management Review*, 1992, *17*(2), 183–211.

25. For more on this topic, see J. M. Kouzes and B. Z. Posner, *The Leadership Challenge*, 4th ed. (San Francisco: Jossey-Bass, 2007), pp. 199–211.

26. Bandura, "Conclusion," pp. 327–328. See also R. F. Mager, "No Self-Efficacy, No Performance," *Training*, April 1992, pp. 32–35.

27. B. Z. Posner and L. M. Brown, "Exploring the Relationship Between Learning and Leadership," *Leadership and Organization Development Journal*, 2001, *22*(6), 274–280; and B. Z. Posner, "Understanding

the Learning Tactics of College Students and Their Relationship to Leadership," *Leadership and Organization Development Journal*, 2009, *30*(4), 386–395.

28. M. Csikszentmihalyi, *Flow: The Psychology of Optimal Experience* (New York: HarperCollins, 1990), pp. 209–213.

29. For another discussion of the makeup of character see Lickona, *Educating for Character*, p. 51.

Chapter Four: Appreciate Constituents

1. J. P. Kotter and J. L. Heskett, *Corporate Culture and Performance* (New York: Free Press, 1992), p. 143.

2. Learning International, "Profiles in Customer Loyalty: An Industry-by-Industry Examination of Buyer-Seller Relationships" (Stamford, CT: Learning International, 1989).

3. See, for example, B. Z. Posner, "Person-Organization Values Congruence: No Support for Individual Differences as a Moderating Influence," *Human Relations*, 1992, *45*(2), 351–361; B. Z. Posner, "Another Look at the Impact of Personal and Organizational Values Congruency," *Journal of Business Ethics*, 2010, *97*(4), 535–541; B. Z. Posner, J. M. Kouzes, and W. H. Schmidt, "Shared Values Make a Difference: An Empirical Test of Corporate Culture," *Human Resource Management*, 1985, *24*(3), 293–310; B. Z. Posner, W. A. Randolph, and W. H. Schmidt, "Managerial Values Across Finance, Manufacturing, Marketing, and Personnel: Some Similarities and Differences," *International Journal of Value-Based Management*, 1993, *6*(2), 19–30; B. Z. Posner and W. H. Schmidt, "Demographic Characteristics and Shared Values," *International Journal of Value-Based Management*, 1992, *5*(1), 77–87; B. Z. Posner and W. H. Schmidt, "Values Congruence and Differences Between the Interplay of Personal and Organizational Value Systems," *Journal of Business Ethics*, 1993, *12*, 341–347; and B. Z. Posner and R. I. Westwood, "A Cross-Cultural Investigation of the Shared Values

Relationship," *International Journal of Value-Based Management*, 1995, *8*, 197–206.

4. A. Argandona, "Fostering Values in Organizations," *Journal of Business Ethics*, 2003, *45*(1), 15–48.

5. For the most recent report, see B. Z. Posner, "Values and the American Manager: A Three-Decade Perspective," *Journal of Business Ethics*, 2010, *91*(4), 457–465. Previous studies include W. H. Schmidt and B. Z. Posner, *Managerial Values and Expectations: The Silent Power in Personal and Organizational Life* (New York: American Management Association, 1982); W. H. Schmidt and B. Z. Posner, "Values and Expectations of Federal Service Executives," *Public Administration Review*, 1986, *46*(5), 447–454; and B. Z. Posner and W. H. Schmidt, "Values and the American Manager: An Update Updated," *California Management Review*, 1992, *34*(3), 80–94.

6. Posner, "Values and the American Manager: A Three-Decade Perspective."

7. Posner, "Another Look at the Impact of Personal and Organizational Values Congruency."

8. When the values of the sons and daughters of the stereotypical "Organization Man" profiled in the book by the same name in the mid-1950s were examined, a similar conclusion was reached. P. Leinberger and B. Tucker, *The New Individualists: The Generation After the Organization Man* (New York: HarperCollins, 1991).

9. R. T. Moran, P. R. Harris, and S. V. Moran, *Managing Cultural Differences: Global Leadership Strategies for the 21st Century*, 7th ed. (Burlington, MA: Elsevier, 2007); and S. E. Page, *The Difference: How the Power of Diversity Creates Better Groups, Firms, Schools, and Societies* (Princeton, NJ: Princeton University Press, 2007).

10. R. R. Thomas Jr., *Building on the Promise of Diversity: How We Can Move to the Next Level in Our Workplaces, Our Communities, and Our Society* (New York: AMACOM, 2006); and R. D. Bucher, *Diversity Consciousness: Opening Our Minds to People, Cultures, and Opportunities*, 3rd ed. (Upper Saddle River, NJ: Prentice Hall, 2009).

11. B. B. Bunker, "Appreciating Diversity and Modifying Organizational Cultures: Men and Women at Work," in *Appreciative Management and Leadership* (rev. ed.), edited by S. Srivastva, D. L. Cooperrider, and Associates (Brunswick, OH: Crown Custom, 1999), pp. 126–149.

12. R. Fisher and S. Brown, *Getting Together* (Boston: Houghton Mifflin, 1988); J. E. Dutton, *Energize Your Workplace: How to Create and Sustain High-Quality Connections at Work* (San Francisco: Jossey-Bass, 2003); C. L. Wall, *The Courage to Trust: A Guide to Developing Deep and Lasting Relationships* (Oakland, CA: New Harbinger, 2005); and J. E. Dutton and B. R. Ragins (Eds.), *Exploring Positive Relationships at Work: Building a Theoretical and Research Foundation* (London: Psychology Press, 2006).

13. M. W. McCall, M. Lombardo, and A. Morrison, *The Lessons of Experience* (Lexington, MA.: Lexington Books, 1988); T. Irwin, *Derailed: Five Lessons Learned from Catastrophic Failures of Leadership* (Nashville: Thomas Nelson, 2009); and J. Collins, *How the Mighty Fall: And Why Some Companies Never Give In* (New York: HarperCollins, 2009).

14. S. Srivastva and F. J. Barrett, "Foundations for Executive Integrity: Dialogue, Diversity, Development," in *Executive Integrity*, edited by S. Srivastva and Associates (San Francisco: Jossey-Bass, 1988), pp. 308.

15. C. Li, *Open Leadership: How Social Technology Can Transform the Way You Lead* (San Francisco: Jossey-Bass, 2010), pp. xiii–xiv. See also M. Fraser and R. Berger, *Throwing Sheep in the Boardroom: How Online Social Networking Will Change Your Life, Work, and World* (Hoboken, NJ: Wiley, 2009).

16. M. Fraser and S. Dutta, "Yes, CEOs Should Facebook and Twitter," Forbes.com, March 11, 2009, accessed online at www.forbes.com/2009 /03/11/social-networking-executives-leadership-managing-facebook .html on November 15, 2010.

17. D. G. Mulhern, private conversation, November 14, 2010. See D. G. Mulhern, *Everyday Leadership: Getting Results in Business, Politics and Life* (Ann Arbor: University of Michigan Press, 2007); also see his website, www.danmulhern.com.

18. According to author Malcolm Gladwell, social media technologies promote "weak ties," but when it comes to major change "strong ties" are needed. "The instruments of social media are well suited to making the existing social order more efficient," but not well suited to systemic change. See M. Gladwell, "Small Change: Why the Revolution Will Not Be Tweeted," *New Yorker*, October 4, 2010, p. 6, accessed online at www.newyorker.com/reporting/2010/10/04/101004fa_fact_gladwell?printable=true&currentPage=all on November 15, 2010.

19. See, for example, D. Jamieson and J. O'Mara, *Managing Workforce 2000: Gaining the Diversity Advantage* (San Francisco: Jossey-Bass, 1991); A. Phatak, R. Bhagat, and R. Kashlak, *International Management: Managing in a Diverse and Dynamic Global Environment*, 2nd ed. (New York: McGraw-Hill/Irwin, 2008); A. C. Edmondson, "Managing the Risk of Learning: Psychological Safety in Work Teams," in *International Handbook of Organizational Teamwork and Cooperative Working*, edited by M. A. West, D. Tjosvold, and K. G. Smith (New York: Wiley, 2003); and J. R. Folkman, *The Power of Feedback: 35 Principles for Turning Feedback from Others into Personal and Professional Change* (Hoboken, NJ: Wiley, 2006).

20. J. M. Kouzes and B. Z. Posner, *The Leadership Practices Inventory (LPI)*, 3rd ed. (San Francisco: Pfeiffer, 2003). To access this instrument online go to: www.leadershipchallenge.com/WileyCDA/LCTitle/productCd-PCOL52.html. Also see B. Z. Posner, "Leadership Practices Inventory (LPI) Data Analysis, September 2010," available online at: www.leadershipchallenge.com/WileyCDA/Section/id-131362.

21. J. A. Sniezek and R. A. Henry, "Accuracy and Confidence in Group Judgment," *Organizational Behavior and Human Decision Processes*, 1989, *43*, 1–28; and J. A. Sniezek and R. A. Henry, "Revision, Weighting and Commitment in Consensus Group Judgment," *Organizational Behavior and Human Decision Processes*, 1990, *45*, 66–84.

22. B. Z. Posner, "Individual's Moral Judgment and Its Impact on Group Processes," *International Journal of Management*, 1986, *3*(2), 5–11.

23. W. Bennis, "Leading Followers, Following Leaders," *Executive Excellence*, June 1991, pp. 5–7.

24. See, for example, M. Deutsch, *The Resolution of Conflict* (New Haven, CT: Yale University Press, 1973); D. Tjosvold, "Implications of Controversy Research for Management," *Journal of Management*, 1985, *11*, 21–37; and D. Tjosvold, *Learning to Manage Conflict* (Lanham, MD: Lexington Books, 2000).

25. D. Tjosvold, *The Team Organization* (New York: Wiley, 1992); and D. Tjosvold and M. M. Tjosvold, *Leading the Team Organization* (Lanham, MD: Lexington Books, 1998).

26. A. Schlaefli, J. R. Rest, and S. J. Thoma, "Does Moral Education Improve Moral Judgment? A Meta-Analysis of Intervention Studies Using the Defining Issues Test," *Review of Educational Research*, Fall 1985, *55*(3), 319–352; R. R. Thomas, *Building on the Promise of Diversity: How We Can Move to the Next Level in Our Workplaces, Our Communities, and Our Society* (New York: AMACOM, 2005); R. D. Bucher, *Diversity Consciousness: Opening Our Minds to People, Cultures and Opportunities* (New York: Prentice Hall, 2009); and C. E. Runde and T. A. Flanagan, *Developing Your Conflict Competence: A Hands-On Guide for Leaders, Managers, Facilitators, and Teams* (San Francisco: Jossey-Bass, 2010).

27. J. M. Kouzes and B. Z. Posner, *The Truth About Leadership* (San Francisco: Jossey-Bass, 2010).

28. D. O'Keefe, *Persuasion: Theory and Research,* 2nd ed. (Thousand Oaks, CA: Sage, 2002); Kouzes and Posner, *The Truth About Leadership*.

29. S. Castaldo, K. Premazzi, and F. Zerbini, "The Meaning(s) of Trust: A Content Analysis on the Diverse Conceptualizations of Trust in Scholarly Research on Business Relationships," *Journal of Business Ethics*, 2010, *96*(4), 657–668.

30. A. C. Edmondson, "Managing the Risk of Learning: Psychological Safety in Work Teams," in *International Handbook of Organizational Teamwork and Cooperative Working*, edited by M. A. West, D. Tjosvold, and K. G. Smith (Hoboken, NJ: Wiley, 2003); and A. Carmeli, D. Brueller and J. E. Dutton, "Learning Behaviours in the Workplace: The Role

of High-Quality Interpersonal Relationships and Psychological Safety," *Systems Research and Behavioral Science*, 2009, *26*, 81–98.

31. R. Audi, "Some Dimension of Trust in Business Practices: From Financial and Product Representation to Licensure and Voting," *Journal of Business Ethics*, 2008, *80*(1), 97–102; K. S. Cook, M. Levi, and R. Hardin, *Whom Can We Trust: How Groups, Networks, and Institutions Make Trust Possible* (New York: Russell Sage Foundation, 2009); and C. Caldwell, L. A. Hayes, and D. T. Long, "Leadership, Trustworthiness, and Ethical Stewardship," *Journal of Business Ethics*, 2010, *96*, 497–512.

32. The classic study in this area is D. E. Zand, "Trust and Managerial Problem Solving," *Administrative Science Quarterly*, 1972, *17*(2), 229–239.

33. J. W. Driscoll, "Trust and Participation in Organizational Decision Making as Predictors of Satisfaction," *Academy of Management Journal*, 1978, *21*(1), 44–56.

Chapter Five: Affirm Shared Values

1. Adapted from "Ujima," from Nguzo Saba Films *Teacher's Guide* (San Francisco: Nguzo Saba Films, 1975).

2. B. Z. Posner, "Another Look at the Impact of Personal and Organizational Values Congruency," *Journal of Business Ethics*, 2010, *97*(4), 535–541.

3. See, for example, C. Enz and C. R. Schwenk, "Performance and Sharing of Organizational Values," paper presented at the annual meeting of the Academy of Management, Washington, D.C., August 1989; B. Meglino, E. C. Ravlin, and C. L. Adkins, "A Work Values Approach to Corporate Culture: A Field Test of the Value Congruence Process and Its Relationship to Individual Outcomes," *Journal of Applied Psychology*, 1989, *74*(3), 424–432; C. A. O'Reilly, J. Chatman, and D. Caldwell, "People and Organizational Culture: A Q-Sort Approach to Assessing Person-Organization Fit," *Academy of Management Journal*, 1991, *34*(3), 487–516; P. McDonald and J. Gandz, "Getting Value from Shared

Values," *Organizational Dynamics*, 1992, *38*(4), 64–76; and B. Z. Posner, J. M. Kouzes, and W. H. Schmidt, "Shared Values Make a Difference: An Empirical Test of Corporate Culture," *Human Resource Management*, 1985, *24*(3), 293–310.

4. John W. Gardner, commencement address, Stanford University, June 16, 1991.

5. Ortho Biotech is now Centocor Ortho Biotech, Inc., part of the Johnson & Johnson family of companies. In 2008 Ortho Biotech joined with Centocor, Inc., to form one company.

6. J. M. Kouzes and B. Z. Posner, *The Truth About Leadership* (San Francisco: Jossey-Bass, 2010).

7. J. A. Autry, *Love and Profit: The Art of Caring Leadership* (New York: HarperCollins, 1992), p. 74.

8. See, for example, F. Richter and D. Tjosvold, "Effects of Student Participation in Classroom Decision Making on Attitudes, Peer Interaction, Motivation, and Learning," *Journal of Applied Psychology*, 1981, *65*, 74–80; D. Tjosvold, I. R. Andrews, and H. Jones, "Cooperative and Competitive Relationships Between Leaders and Their Subordinates," *Human Relations*, 1983, *36*, 1111–1124; D. Tjosvold, I. R. Andrews, and H. Jones, "Alternative Ways Leaders Can Use Authority," *Canadian Journal of Administrative Sciences*, 1985, *2*, 307–317; D. Tjosvold, "Power and Social Context in Superior-Subordinate Interaction," *Organizational Behavior and Human Decision Processes*, 1985, *35*, 281–293; and D. Tjosvold, I. R. Andrews, and J. T. Struthers, "Power and Interdependence in Work Groups," *Group and Organization Studies*, 1991, *16*(3), 285–299.

9. D. Tjosvold, "Interdependence and Power Between Managers and Employees: A Study of the Leader Relationship," *Journal of Management*, 1988, *15*, 49–64.

10. A. Kohn, *No Contest: The Case Against Competition*, 2nd ed. (Boston: Houghton Mifflin, 1992).

11. A. Kohn, *The Brighter Side of Human Nature: Altruism and Empathy in Everyday Life* (New York: Basic Books, 1990).

12. R. Levering, presentation to the Bay Area Ethics Consortium, Berkeley, CA., January 30, 1991. Also see Amy Lyman, "Creating Trust: It's Worth the Effort," Great Place to Work Institute, 2008, accessed online at www.greatplacetowork.com/news/articles.php on October 17, 2010.

13. The 100 Best Companies to Work For is an annual listing in *Fortune* magazine of those organizations that receive the highest ratings on the Great Place to Work Trust Index, a proprietary survey developed by the Great Place to Work Institute. The Trust Index measures credibility, respect, fairness, pride, and camaraderie. For more information about recent winners as well as the process visit the Great Place to Work Institute online at www.greatplacetowork.com.

14. For a complete list of the principles in Google's philosophy, visit the Google Inc. website: www.google.com/corporate/tenthings.html.

15. T. Hsieh, *Delivering Happiness: A Path to Profits, Passion, and Purpose* (New York: Business Plus, 2010), p. 134. The *Culture Book* came about as a result of a conversation CEO Tony Hsieh was having with employees one evening: "There was a group of us hanging out one night talking about how we could make sure that we continued to hire only people who would fit into the Zappos culture. There was a new hire in the group, so I asked each person to talk about the Zappos culture." After everyone had given their own interpretations, Tony remarked that he wished they had recorded the conversation so they could share it with all new hires. He then blurted out, "You know what? We should just ask *all* our employees to write a few paragraphs about what the Zappos culture means to them, and compile it all into a book" (p. 134).

16. To learn more about the Zappos culture visit http://blogs.zappos.com. To order a copy of the *Culture Book*, send an e-mail to ceo@zappos.com containing your physical mailing address. If you are thinking this might be something useful to do, reflect on these questions from Jenn Lim, the person Tony turned to for help in compiling the first *Culture Book*: "Would you be comfortable printing everything your employees, customers, and partners have to say about your culture? If not, what

would it take for you to get there? No culture book is worth much unless it reflects culture and values that are already in place" (Hsieh, *Delivering Happiness*, p. 137).

17. "Joining the Team: Getting Oriented at Qualcomm," Great Place to Work Institute, 2007, available online at www.greatplacetowork .com/news/articles.php.

18. "Qualcomm Social Responsibility Report 2008," Qualcomm, 2009, p. 22, available online at www.qualcomm.com/documents/csr-report-2008.

19. M. Weinstein, "A Day in the Life at DaVita Academy," *managesmarter*, January 6, 2010, accessed online at www.trainingmag.com/article/day-life-davita-academy, January 27, 2011.

20. A. Gostick and C. Elton, *Managing with Carrots: Using Recognition to Attract and Retain the Best People* (Salt Lake City, UT: Gibbs-Smith, 2001), p. 16; also see A. Gostick and C. Elton, *The Carrot Principle: How the Best Managers Use Recognition to Engage Their People, Retain Talent, and Accelerate Performance* (New York: Free Press, 2009).

21. C. Conley, *Peak: How Great Companies Get Their Mojo from Maslow* (San Francisco: Jossey-Bass, 2007), pp. 68–69.

22. For more on Yum! Awards (and a look at the chomping dentures), see www.yum.com/company/recognition.asp.

23. The Netflix statement is available online at www.slideshare.net/reed2001/culture-1798664.

24. "Six in Ten Say Recession Has Harmed Their Own Company's Culture," Ipsos press release, October 4, 2010, accessed online at www.ipsos-na.com/news-polls/pressrelease.aspx?id=4980 on October 9, 2010.

25. W. Ury, *Getting Past No,* rev. ed. (New York: Bantam Books, 1993), p. 29. Also see A. Maravelas, *How to Reduce Workplace Conflict and Stress: How Leaders and Their Employees Can Protect Their Sanity and Productivity from Tension and Turf Wars* (Franklin Lakes, NJ: Career Press, 2005); and W. Ury, *The Power of a Positive No: Save the Deal, Save the Relationship—and Still Say No* (New York: Bantam Books, 2008).

26. C. Hampden-Turner, *Charting the Corporate Mind: Graphic Solutions to Business Conflicts* (New York: Free Press, 1990), p. 7.

27. R. Fisher and S. Brown, *Getting Together: Building a Relationship That Gets to Yes* (Boston: Houghton Mifflin, 1988), p. 37.

Chapter Six: Develop Capacity

1. G. Colvin, "How Are Most Admired Companies Different? They Invest in People and Keep Them Employed—Even in a Downturn," *Fortune*, March 28, 2010, p. 38.

2. Colvin, "How Are Most Admired Companies Different?"

3. R. Zhang and Z. Rezaee, "Do Credible Firms Perform Better in Emerging Markets? Evidence from China," *Journal of Business Ethics*, 2009, *90*, 221–237.

4. This example was provided from Claria Guo's "most admired leader" essay.

5. A. P. Carnevale, *America and the New Economy: How New Competitive Standards Are Radically Changing American Workplaces* (San Francisco: Jossey-Bass, 1991); A. P. Carnevale, private e-mail message to James M. Kouzes, November 18, 2010. Also see C. I. Jones, "Sources of U.S. Economic Growth in a World of Ideas," *American Economic Review,* 2002, *92*(1), 220–239; and C. Goldin and L. F. Katz, *The Race Between Education and Technology* (Cambridge, MA: Harvard University Press, 2008).

6. S. Crabtree, "How to Bolster Employees' Confidence," *Gallup Management Journal*, February 25, 2010, accessed online at http://gmj.gallup.com/content/126173/bolster-employees-confidence.aspx on August 13, 2010.

7. "Building Organizational Capabilities: McKinsey Global Survey Results," *McKinsey Quarterly*, March 2010, accessed online at https://www.mckinseyquarterly.com/Building_organizational_capabilities_McKinsey_Global_Survey_results_2540 on August 13, 2010.

8. "Building Organizational Capabilities."

9. J. Stack, *The Great Game of Business* (New York: Doubleday, 1992), pp. 15–16. Also see J. Stack, *A Stake in the Outcome: Building a Culture of Ownership for the Long-Term Success of Your Business* (New York: Doubleday, 2003); and J. Stack, "It's More Than Just Opening the Books," *New York Times Online*, June 7, 2010, accessed online at http://boss.blogs.nytimes.com/2010/06/07/its-more-than-just-opening-the-books/ on August 13, 2010.

10. See, for example, L. A. Schlesinger and J. Zornitsky, "Job Satisfaction, Service Capability, and Customer Satisfaction: An Examination of Their Linkages and Management Implications," *Human Resource Planning*, Spring 1991; and L. A. Schlesinger and J. L. Heskett, "Enfranchisement of Service Workers," *California Management Review*, Summer 1991, pp. 83–100.

11. E. L. Deci, *Why We Do What We Do: Understanding Self-Motivation* (New York: Penguin Books, 1996); also see K. W. Thomas, *Intrinsic Motivation at Work: Building Energy and Commitment*, 2nd ed. (San Francisco: Berrett-Koehler, 2009).

12. R. E. Wood and A. Bandura, "Impact of Conceptions of Ability on Self-Regulatory Mechanisms and Complex Decision Making," *Journal of Personality and Social Psychology*, 1989, *56*, 407–415.

13. A. Bandura and R. E. Wood, "Effect of Perceived Controllability and Performance Standards on Self-Regulation of Complex Decision Making," *Journal of Personality and Social Psychology*, 1989, *56*, 805–814.

14. J. M. Kouzes and B. Z. Posner, *The Truth About Leadership* (San Francisco: Jossey-Bass, 2010), pp. 75–89. See also R. B. Shaw, *Trust in the Balance: Building Successful Organizations on Results, Integrity, and Concern* (San Francisco: Jossey-Bass, 1997); and J. Hamm, *Unusual Excellence* (San Francisco: Jossey-Bass, 2011).

15. C. S. Dweck, *Mindset: The New Psychology of Success* (New York: Random House, 2006), p. 7.

16. Dweck, *Mindset*.

17. Kouzes and Posner, *The Truth About Leadership*, pp. 119–133.

219

18. E. J. Langer, *Mindfulness* (Reading, MA: Addison-Wesley, 1989); and *The Power of Mindful Learning* (New York: Perseus Books, 1998).

19. E. J. Langer and A. Piper, "The Prevention of Mindlessness," *Journal of Personality and Social Psychology*, 1987, *53*, 280–287; also see Langer, *Mindfulness*, p. 120.

20. Psychologist Ellen Langer at Harvard describes a similar experiment involving schoolchildren. In one classroom, she showed a picture of a person in a wheelchair and asked, "Can this person drive a car?" The students uniformly answered no, and they had no trouble coming up with reasons why. This was not a very constructive conversation. In another classroom, she showed the same picture and asked a slightly different question, "How can this person drive a car?" After some silence, the students started to offer ideas. A whole different kind of conversation ensued—creative, energized, and constructive. Langer, *Mindfulness*, pp. 168–169.

21. "Capitalizing on Complexity: Insights from the Global Chief Executive Officer Study, 2010," accessed online at http://ibm.com/capitalizingoncomplexity on August 14, 2010.

22. C. Wang, *Managerial Decision Making and Leadership* (Hoboken, NJ: Wiley, 2010).

23. V. Nayer, *Employees First, Customers Second: Turning Conventional Management Upside Down* (Cambridge: Harvard Business Press, 2010).

24. A. Kleiner and V. Sehgal, "Thought Leader: Vineet Nayar," *Strategy + Business*, October 18, 2010, p. 5, accessed online at www.strategy-business.com/article/10410?pg=all on January 5, 2011.

25. A. Bandura and D. Cervone, "Self-Evaluative and Self-Efficacy Mechanisms Governing the Motivational Effects of Goal Systems," *Journal of Personality and Social Psychology*, 1983, *45*, 1017–1028.

26. R. Henkoff, "Make Your Office More Productive," *Fortune*, February 25, 1991, p. 82.

27. Bandura and Cervone, "Self-Evaluative and Self-Efficacy Mechanisms."

Chapter Seven: Serve a Purpose

1. "On Leadership: Ford CEO Alan Mulally on the 'Liberating Clarity' of His Mission," *Washington Post on Leadership*, www.views.washingtonpost.com/leadership, February 16, 2010, accessed online at www.washingtonpost.com/wp-dyn/content/video/2010/03/17/VI2010 031700383.html on August 16, 2010. Also see P. Kaipa and M. Kriger, "Empowerment, Vision, and Positive Leadership: An Interview with Alan Mulally, Former CEO, Boeing Commercial—Current CEO, Ford Motor Company," *Journal of Management Inquiry*, 2010, *19*(2), 110–115.

2. R. K. Greenleaf, *Servant Leadership: A Journey into the Nature of Legitimate Power and Greatness* (New York: Paulist Press, 1977), p. 7.

3. Greenleaf, *Servant Leadership*, p. 10.

4. C. Li, *Open Leadership: How Social Technology Can Transform the Way You Lead* (San Francisco: Jossey-Bass, 2010), p. 14.

5. J. M. Kouzes and B. Z. Posner, *The Truth About Leadership* (San Francisco: Jossey-Bass, 2010), pp. 105–118.

6. C. W. Berger, presentation at the Leavey School of Business, Santa Clara University, October 1, 2010.

7. T. Simons, *The Integrity Dividend* (San Francisco: Jossey-Bass, 2008).

8. T. Peters, *The Little Big Things: 163 Ways to Pursue Excellence* (New York: HarperBusiness, 2010), p. 481.

9. For an excellent discussion of how leaders reinforce and serve shared values to transmit organizational culture, see E. H. Schein, *Organizational Culture and Leadership*, 4th ed. (San Francisco: Jossey-Bass, 2010), pp. 235–258.

10. L. Wiseman with G. McKeown, *Multipliers: How the Best Leaders Make Everyone Smarter* (New York: HarperBusiness, 2010), p. 79.

11. See C. Heath and D. Heath, *Made to Stick: Why Some Ideas Survive and Others Don't* (New York: Random House, 2007), pp. 204–237.

12. See, for example, E. Borgida and R. E. Nisbett, "The Differential Impact of Abstract vs. Concrete Information on Decisions," *Journal of Applied Technology*, 1977, *7*(3), 258–271; A. L. Wilkens, "Organizational Stories as Symbols Which Control the Organization," in *Organizational Symbolism,* edited by L. R. Pondy, P. J. Frost, G. Morgan, and T. C. Dandridge (Greenwich, CT: JAI Press, 1983); R. Zemke, "Storytelling: Back to Basic," *Training*, March 1990, pp. 44–50; P. Schwartz, *The Art of the Long View* (New York: Doubleday, 1991); J. A. Conger, "Inspiring Others: The Language of Leadership," *Academy of Management Executive*, 1991, *5*(1), 38; and S. Denning, *The Secret Language of Leadership: How Leaders Inspire Action Through Narrative* (San Francisco: Jossey-Bass, 2007).

13. J. A. Conger, "Inspiring Others," p. 38.

14. D. M. Armstrong, *Managing by Storying Around: A New Method of Leadership* (New York: Doubleday, 1992), pp. 7–9.

15. S. Taylor and L. Novelli Jr., "Some Basic Concepts of Innovation and Story Telling," *Issues and Observation*, 1991, *11*(1), 6–9. See also S. Denning, *The Leader's Guide to Storytelling: Mastering the Art and Discipline of Business Narrative* (San Francisco: Jossey-Bass, 2005).

16. This example was provided by Jacqueline Wong in her "My Most Admired Leader" essay.

17. L. L. Berry and A. Parasuraman, *Marketing Services: Competing Through Quality* (New York: Free Press, 1991), p. 38.

18. For further discussion of the steps in service recovery, see C. R. Bell and R. Zemke, *Managing Knock Your Socks Off Service*, 2nd ed. (New York: AMACOM, 2007); and R. Zemke and C. R. Bell, *Knock Your Socks Off Service Recovery* (New York: AMACOM, 2000). Also see D. Reina and M. Reina, *Rebuilding Trust in the Workplace* (San Francisco: Berrett-Koehler, 2010).

Chapter Eight: Sustain Hope

1. Our research clearly shows that managers who are dynamic and inspiring are significantly more credible than managers who are not.

2. This example was originally contributed by Pierfrancesco Ronzi. Further information about *Shosholoza* can be found on www .thesailingchannel.tv/sailtv/videos/shosholoza.htm, viewed August 31, 2010.

3. For a video on the program, see www.teamshosholoza.com/shosholoza_ uphi/main.htm?sb=0, viewed June 2, 2010.

4. C. R. Snyder, *The Psychology of Hope: You Can Get Here from There* (New York: Free Press, 2003). Also see C. R. Snyder, C. Harris, J. R. Anderson, S. A. Holleran, L. M. Irving, S. T. Sigmon, L. Yoshinobu, J. Gibb, C. Langelle, and P. Harney, "The Will and the Ways: Development and Validation of an Individual-Differences Measure of Hope," *Journal of Personality and Social Psychology*, 1991, *60*(4), 570–585.

5. See T. R. Elliott, T. E. Witty, and S. Herrick, "Negotiating Reality After Physical Loss: Hope, Depression, and Disability," *Journal of Personality and Social Psychology*, 1991, *61*(4), 608–613. Also see D. Goleman, "In New Research, Optimism Emerges as the Key to a Successful Life," *New York Times*, December 24, 1991, pp. B1–B6.

6. C. Peterson and L. M. Bossio, *Health and Optimism: New Research on the Relationship Between Positive Thinking and Physical Well-Being* (New York: Free Press, 1991), p. 30.

7. See J. Talan, "Optimism May Be the Best Medicine," *San Jose Mercury News*, May 22, 1991, pp. 1F, 3F. For research on health and optimism, see Peterson and Bossio, *Health and Optimism*. Also see M.E.P. Seligman, *Learned Optimism: How to Change Your Mind and Your Life* (New York: Vintage, 2006).

8. S. Walton with J. Huey, *Sam Walton: Made in America—My Story* (New York: Doubleday, 1992), p. 30.

9. N. Cousins, *Head First: The Biology of Hope* (New York: Dutton, 1989), p. 83.

10. For a more extensive treatment of the attitudes of psychologically hardy individuals, see S. R. Maddi and D. M. Khoshaba, *Resilience at Work: How to Succeed No Matter What Life Throws at You* (New York: AMACOM, 2005); and S. R. Maddi and S. C. Kobasa, *The Hardy Executive: Health Under Stress* (Chicago: Dorsey Professional Books/Dow Jones-Irwin,

1984). For more on the attitudes and practices of resilient people, especially those who overcome abusive childhoods, see S. Wolin and S. Wolin, quoted in "How to Survive (Practically) Anything," *Psychology Today*, January/February 1992; S. Wolin and S. Wolin, *Resilience: How Survivors of Troubled Families Rise Above Adversity* (New York: Villard, 1993); T. Rogers, "Why Some People Transcend Their Traumatic Childhoods," *San Francisco Chronicle*, January 2, 1991, p. B3; and R. B. Flannery Jr., *Becoming Stress-Resistant Through the SMART Program* (New York: Continuum, 1990).

11.   Quoted in Goleman, "In New Research, Optimism Emerges." Also see Snyder, *The Psychology of Hope*, p. 5.

12.   A. L. Duckworth, C. Peterson, M. D. Matthews, and D. R. Kelly, "Personality Processes and Individual Differences," *Journal of Personality and Social Psychology*, 2007, *92*(6), 1087–1088.

13.   J. Lehrer, "The Truth About Grit: Modern Science Builds Case for an Old-Fashioned Virtue—and Uncovers New Secrets to Success," *Boston Globe*, accessed at www.boston.com/bostonglobe/ideas/articles/2009/08/02/the_truth_about_grit/ on January 27, 2011.

14.   R. M. Brown, "Rita Mae Brown," in *The Courage of Conviction*, edited by P. L. Berman (New York: Dodd, Mead, 1985), p. 23.

15.   Brown, "Rita Mae Brown," p. 23.

16.   For a discussion of optimal performance and the issue of balance of challenge and skill, see M. Csikszentmihalyi, *Flow: The Psychology of Optimal Performance* (New York: Free Press, 1990).

17.   See Goleman, "In New Research, Optimism Emerges." Also see Snyder and others, "The Will and the Ways."

18.   See Wolin and Wolin, "How to Survive (Practically) Anything"; and Flannery, *Becoming Stress-Resistant*.

19.   See J. M. Kouzes and B. Z. Posner, *The Leadership Challenge*, 4th ed. (San Francisco: Jossey-Bass, 2007), pp. 79–130.

20.   For a discussion of group effectiveness and positive images, see D. L. Cooperrider, "Positive Image, Positive Action: The Affirmative Basis of Organizing," in *Appreciative Management and Leadership: The Power*

of Positive Thought and Action in Organizations, edited by S. Srivastva, D. L. Cooperrider, and Associates (San Francisco: Jossey-Bass, 1990), pp. 108, 115. For the original study on group images, see R. Schwartz, "The Internal Dialogue: On the Asymmetry Between Positive and Negative Coping Thoughts," *Cognitive Therapy and Research*, 1986, *10*, 591–605.

21. F. Polak, *The Image of the Future* (New York: Elsevier, 1973), p. 19. Quoted in Cooperrider, "Positive Image, Positive Action," p. 111.

22. J. McCarthy, "Short Stories and Tall Tales at Work: Organizational Storytelling as a Leadership Conduit During Turbulent Times," doctoral dissertation, Boston University, 2002.

23. B. L. Fredrickson, *Positivity: Groundbreaking Research Reveals How to Embrace the Hidden Strengths of Positive Emotions, Overcome Negativity, and Thrive* (New York: Crown, 2009), p. 21.

24. Fredrickson, *Positivity*, pp. 60–65.

25. For studies on the health effects of optimism, see Peterson and Bossio, *Health and Optimism*. For a detailed discussion of how optimism assessment and training have been used to increase sales performance, see Seligman, *Learned Optimism*.

26. Seligman, *Learned Optimism*.

27. Goleman, "In New Research, Optimism Emerges," p. B6.

28. See Seligman, *Learned Optimism*, pp. 93–204.

29. See R. Boyatzis and A. McKee, *Resonant Leadership* (Boston: Harvard Business Press, 2005), pp. 147–174. See also Fredrickson, *Positivity*.

30. Seligman, *Learned Optimism*, p. 109.

31. This example was originally contributed by Hilary Hall. Further information about Mindy Grossman is available in A. Bryant, "Are You a Tigger, or an Eeyore?" *New York Times*, November 15, 2009, p. B42.

32. J. H. Bryant, *Love Leadership: The New Way to Lead in a Fear-Based World* (San Francisco: Jossey-Bass, 2009), p. 31.

33. Bryant, *Love Leadership*, p. 13.

34. P. L. Townsend, "Love and Leadership," *Marine Corps Gazette*, February 1982, p. 24.

35. J. Autry, *Love and Profit: The Art of Caring Leadership* (New York: Morrow, 1991).

36. R. J. Sternberg and S. Grajeck, "The Nature of Love," *Journal of Personality and Social Psychology*, 1984, *47*(2), 327.

Chapter Nine: The Struggle to Be Human

1. In our book *The Truth About Leadership* (San Francisco: Jossey-Bass, 2010) we report that the two questions people most want their leaders to answer are: (1) Who are you? and (2) Where are we going?

2. K. E. Weick and K. M. Sutcliffe, *Managing the Unexpected: Resilient Performance in an Age of Uncertainty,* 2nd ed. (San Francisco: Jossey-Bass, 2007); and M. S. Malone, *The Future Arrived Yesterday: The Rise of the Protean Corporation and What It Means for You* (New York: Crown, 2009).

3. This point is being made by such notable thinkers as Gary Hamel, *The Future of Management* (Boston: Harvard Business Press, 2007); Thomas Friedman, *The World Is Flat—Release 3.0: A Brief History of the Twenty-First Century* (New York: Farrar, Straus & Giroux, 2007); and Noel Tichy and Warren Bennis, *Judgment: How Winning Leaders Make Great Calls* (New York: Portfolio/Penguin, 2007).

4. M. J. Adler and W. Gorman (Eds.), *The Great Ideas: A Syntopicon of Great Books of the Western World*, vol. 2 (Chicago: Encyclopedia Britannica, 1952), p. 1337.

5. The company in this story did miss a significant market opportunity and suffered financially.

6. For more information on cognitive complexity, see J. M. Bartunek, J. R. Gordon, and R. P. Weathersby, "Developing 'Complicated' Understanding in Administrators," *Academy of Management Review*, 1983, *8*(2), 273–284. See also S. Coats and T. Heuer, *There Is No Box* (Provo, UT: Executive Excellence Publishing, 2006); K. Douglas, *The Firefly Effect: Build Teams That Capture Creativity and Catapult Results* (Hoboken, NJ: Wiley, 2009); and S. Joni and D. Beyer, *The Right Fight: How*

Great Leaders Use Healthy Conflict to Drive Performance, Innovation, and Value (New York: HarperCollins, 2010).

7. I. L. Janis, *Victims of Groupthink* (Boston: Houghton Mifflin, 1972), p. 57. Also see R. S. Baron, "So Right It's Wrong: Groupthink and the Ubiquitous Nature of Polarized Group Decision Making," in *Advances in Experimental Social Psychology*, vol. 37 (San Diego: Elsevier Academic Press, 2005), pp. 219–255; J. Surowiecki, *The Wisdom of Crowds* (New York: Random House, 2005); and M. A. Roberto, *Why Great Leaders Don't Take Yes for an Answer: Managing for Conflict and Consensus* (Upper Saddle River, NJ: Pearson Education, 2009).

8. G. Leonard, *Mastery: The Keys to Success and Long-Term Fulfillment* (New York: Dutton, 1991), p. 138.

9. Leonard, *Mastery*, p. 140.

10. D. N. Michael, "The Possible Society: An Exploration of Practical Policy Alternatives for the Decade Ahead," symposium proceedings, National Institute of Public Affairs, April 26–28, 1979, p. 17. This paper was based on an earlier work by the author: D. N. Michael, *On Learning to Plan—And Planning to Learn* (San Francisco: Jossey-Bass, 1973), p. 18.

11. Michael, "The Possible Society," pp. 18–20; and *On Learning to Plan—And Planning to Learn*, p. 18.

12. J. W. Gardner, *On Leadership* (New York: Free Press, 1990), p. 122.

13. Gardner, *On Leadership*, p. 136.

Epilogue: Character Counts

1. Thomas Lickona introduced us to this anonymous verse in a lecture he delivered at Santa Clara University's Markkula Center for Applied Ethics, February 22, 2001.

ACKNOWLEDGMENTS

Our own credibility would be in doubt if we didn't right up front make two acknowledgments: we couldn't have done this alone, and if there are any errors or shortcomings in the manuscript they are our responsibility.

This edition was nearly thirty years in the making, considering that it really first began as the second chapter of our first book, *The Leadership Challenge*. *Credibility* became our second leadership book in the early 1990s. (We've now written over thirty other books, training guides, instruments, monographs, and videos). We're grateful to the millions of people around the world who have purchased our books and materials, completed the Leadership Practices Inventory (LPI), and participated in The Leadership Challenge Workshops. They give us reason, and encouragement, to continue to do our part in liberating the leader within each and every person, and in making extraordinary things possible.

We would also like to thank our collaborators in the research— those who participated in our classes, workshops, and seminars, who completed our surveys, and who were gracious in sharing their case studies and interviews with us. They are the heart and soul of this book. Their stories and examples bring the numbers and qualities to life.

We learned years ago that experience is the best teacher of leadership; their histories reinforce this axiom.

This edition is the direct result of the ongoing support and encouragement of the team at Jossey-Bass/Wiley Publishing. They took the chance that two little-known educators and scholars could make a contribution to the understanding and practice of leadership, and through the years their own engagement in the *Five Practices of Exemplary Leadership* has resulted in an amazing collaboration for the Kouzes Posner franchise. Cedric Crocker, vice president and publisher (Jossey-Bass and Pfeiffer imprints), has been working with us since the beginning. It's been our good fortune and pleasure to have worked with Lisa Shannon, associate publisher, for nearly two decades, and her leadership and genius have enriched our thinking and enhanced our ability to play a major role in developing leaders worldwide. This edition has benefited from the craftsmanship and gentle guidance of Byron Schneider, senior developmental editor, Jossey-Bass, and the careful attention and insightfulness of Karen Murphy, senior editor, Jossey-Bass. We especially want to thank our developmental editor, Leslie Stephen, who brought clarity and focus to our writing, challenged our thinking, and willingly broke ties when we got ourselves bogged down.

Others at Jossey-Bass/Wiley who helped us bring this book into, and through, production and onto bookshelves that deserve special recognition include Mark Karmendy, editorial production manager; Hilary Powers, copyeditor; Gayle Mak, senior editorial assistant; Carolyn Carlstroem, marketing manager; and Amy Packard, publicity manager. Another special note of thanks for her continuing support and encouragement goes out to Debra Hunter, president, Jossey-Bass and Pfieffer.

We want to extend a special thank-you to Stephen DeKrey, senior associate dean of the Business School at the Hong Kong University of Science and Technology, and Nakiye Boyacigiller, dean of the

Faculty of Management at Sabanci University in Istanbul, Turkey. Steve provided Barry with the opportunity to serve as a visiting professor in fall 2009, and Nakiye provided a similar opportunity in spring 2010. These experiences expanded firsthand our global view of leadership.

We also want to give a "shout out" to all of those who made the first edition of this book possible through their generous help, able assistance, and gracious support: Julianne Balmain, Myra Cake, Brian and Anne Carroll, Paul Cohen, Cedric Crocker, Kathy Dalle-Molle, Ray Dallin, Marcella Friel, Bill Hicks, Jerry Hunt, Jan Hunter, JoAnn Johnson, Peter Jordan, Steve Katten, Sarah Kidd, Andre and Barbara Morkel, Trish O'Hare, Lynne Parode, Tom Peters, Debra Scates, Natalie Sibert, Laura Simonds, Tracey Taylor, Janice Van Collie, Francessa Webb, Terri Armstrong Welch, and Barbara Wheeler.

Writing is at once a very lonely pursuit and a very intimate one. Our spouses see us at our most frustrated and our most elated. They hear our constant complaining and our nonstop jabbering about this idea and that—or, at times, even about one another. They have been ever patient, understanding, and supportive. *Credibility* is really their book, too. Our forever thanks and our love to Tae Moon Kouzes and Jackie Schmidt-Posner.

James M. Kouzes
Barry Z. Posner
May 2011

ABOUT THE AUTHORS

Jim Kouzes and Barry Posner are coauthors of the award-winning and best-selling *The Leadership Challenge*. Since its first edition in 1987, *The Leadership Challenge* has sold over two million copies worldwide and is available in more than twenty-two languages. It has won numerous awards, including the Critics' Choice Award from the nation's book review editors and the James A. Hamilton Hospital Administrators' Book-of-the-Year Award, and was selected as one of the top ten books on leadership in *The Top 100 Business Books of All Time*. Their 2010 book, *The Truth About Leadership*, was selected by Soundview Executive Books as one of the best books of the year.

Jim and Barry have coauthored more than a dozen other award-winning leadership books, including *A Leader's Legacy* (selected by Soundview Executive Book Summaries as one of the top thirty books of the year and by the *Globe and Mail* as one of the top ten books of 2006), *Encouraging the Heart, The Student Leadership Challenge*, and *The Academic Administrator's Guide to Exemplary Leadership*. They also developed the highly acclaimed Leadership Practices Inventory (LPI), a 360-degree questionnaire for assessing leadership behavior, which is one of the most widely used leadership assessment instruments in the world, along with The Student LPI. More than 500 doctoral dissertations and academic research projects have been based on their Five Practices of Exemplary Leadership model.

Among the honors and awards that Jim and Barry have received is the American Society for Training and Development's highest award, for Distinguished Contribution to Workplace Learning and Performance. The authors have been named Management/Leadership Educators of the Year by the International Management Council, ranked by *Leadership Excellence* magazine in the top twenty on its list of the Top 100 Thought Leaders, and named among the Top 50 Leadership Coaches in the nation (according to *Coaching for Leadership*). And in 2010 they were listed among *HR Magazine*'s Most Influential International Thinkers and Trust Across America's Top Thought Leaders in Trustworthy Business Behavior.

Jim and Barry are frequent speakers, and each has conducted leadership development programs for hundreds of organizations, including Apple, Applied Materials, ARCO, AT&T, Australia Institute of Management, Australia Post, Bank of America, Bose, Charles Schwab, Cisco Systems, Community Leadership Association, Conference Board of Canada, Consumers Energy, Deloitte Touche, Dorothy Wylie Nursing Leadership Institute, Dow Chemical, Egon Zehnder International, Federal Express, Genentech, Gymboree, Hewlett-Packard, IBM, Intel, Jobs DR-Singapore, Johnson & Johnson, Kaiser Foundation Health Plans and Hospitals, L. L. Bean, Lawrence Livermore National Labs, Lucile Packard Children's Hospital, Merck, Motorola, NetApp, Northrop Grumman, Oracle, Roche Bioscience, Siemens, Standard Aero, 3M, Toyota, the U.S. Postal Service, United Way, USAA, Verizon, VISA, and the Walt Disney Company. They have lectured at more than sixty college and university campuses.

Jim Kouzes is the Dean's Executive Fellow of Leadership, Leavey School of Business, at Santa Clara University, and lectures on leadership around the world to corporations, governments, and nonprofits. He is a highly regarded leadership scholar and an experienced executive, and the *Wall Street Journal* cited him as one of the twelve best executive educators in the United States. In 2010 Jim received the Thought Leadership Award from the Instructional Systems Association, the most prestigious award given by the trade association of training and development industry providers. In 2006 Jim was presented with the Golden Gavel, the highest honor awarded by Toastmasters International. Jim served as president, CEO, and chairman of the Tom Peters Company from 1988 through 1999, and prior to that led the Executive Development Center at Santa Clara University (1981–1987). Jim founded the Joint Center for Human Services Development at San Jose State University (1972–1980) and was on the staff of the School of Social Work, University of Texas. His career in training and development began in 1969 when he conducted seminars for Community Action Agency staff and volunteers in the war on poverty. Following graduation from Michigan State University (BA with honors in political science), he served as a Peace Corps volunteer (1967–1969). Jim can be reached at jim@kouzes.com.

Barry Posner is professor of leadership at the Leavey School of Business, Santa Clara University, where he served as associate dean for graduate education, associate dean for executive education, and dean of the school for twelve years (1997–2009). During the 2009–2010 academic year Barry was a distinguished visiting professor in the fall at Hong Kong University of Science and Technology and in the spring at Sabanci University (Istanbul). At Santa Clara he has received the President's Distinguished Faculty Award, the School's Extraordinary Faculty Award, and several other outstanding teaching and academic honors. An internationally renowned scholar and educator, Barry is author or coauthor of more than a hundred research and practitioner-focused articles. He currently serves on the editorial review boards for *Leadership and Organizational Development, Leadership Review*, and the *International Journal of Servant-Leadership*. In 2011 he received the Outstanding Scholar Award for Career Achievement from the *Journal of Management Inquiry*.

Barry received his BA with honors in political science from the University of California, Santa Barbara, his MA in public administration from The Ohio State University, and his PhD in organizational behavior and administrative theory from the University of Massachusetts, Amherst. Having consulted with a wide variety of public and private sector organizations around the globe, Barry also works at a strategic level with a number of community-based and professional organizations, currently sitting on the board of directors of EMQ FamiliesFirst. He has served previously on the board of the American Institute of Architects, Big Brothers/Big Sisters of Santa Clara County, Center for Excellence in Nonprofits, Junior Achievement of Silicon Valley and Monterey Bay, Public Allies, San Jose Repertory Theater, Sigma Phi Epsilon Fraternity, and several start-up companies. Barry can be reached at bposner@scu.edu.

INDEX

237